Introduction

I N THE 1980s few people thought they would live to see the end of the Cold War, the end of Apartheid in South Africa, or a united government in Northern Ireland. But in less than one decade, all these conflicts did end. The walls came tumbling down because the peacemakers kept hope alive and worked tirelessly to make peace possible.

> For me the struggle is not between Palestinians and Israelis, nor between Jews and Arabs. The fight is between those who seek peace and those who seek war. My people are those who seek peace. My sisters are the bereaved mothers, Israeli and Palestinian, who live in Israel and in Gaza and in the refugee camps. My brothers are the fathers who try to defend their children from the cruel occupation, and are, as I was, unsuccessful in doing so. Although we were born into a different history and speak different tongues, there is more that unites us than that which divides us.

—Nurit Peled Elhanan, an Israeli Jewish mother from Tel Aviv whose 13-year-old daughter was killed by a Palestinian suicide bomber in 1997

Volunteers from Rabbis for Human Rights–Israel (RHR) help Palestinian farmers in the northern West Bank plant trees on land that is now stranded between the Wall and the Green Line.

For over six decades now the bleeding wound inflicted in 1948 in Palestine has gone untreated. In spite of widespread international recognition that an Israeli-Palestinian peace is central to peace in the entire Middle East and beyond, the situation deteriorates further each year. Some draw the conclusion that this conflict is so complex and intractable that peace in our time is impossible. "Nonsense!" say the peacemakers. "Our God is a God of peace, and with God nothing is impossible."

President Barack Obama's bold leadership in changing course from past administrations offers the hopeful prospect of change. At the same time, hope needs to be tempered with caution and realism. It is unwise to underestimate the difficulty of translating hope into reality given Palestinian political fragmentation, a lack of will within the Israeli political structure, and the difficult-to-impossible task of reversing 40-plus years of occupation. Because of the sense that change

may be on the horizon, the content of this book is more timely and relevant than ever. Education and awareness about the history of the conflict, the conditions of occupation, and the patterns that shape the discourse are needed as much now as ever.

The features of occupation described herein provide a yardstick for measuring actual concrete change. While the rhetoric surrounding the conflict may be changing, actual policy has not: no settlers have moved back to Israel, not a meter of the Wall has been removed, and checkpoints continue to paralyze Palestinian movement.

There is a hazard that well-intentioned people will, out of sheer fatigue, be persuaded to support a "solution" that makes them feel better, but does very little to alleviate the situation of the Palestinians and only postpones

Israel's coming to terms with the fact of the continuing Palestinian presence on the land. To raise hope prematurely only contributes to a cycle of false hope and dashed hope that, in the end, leaves observers and participants feeling numb and paralyzed.

Hope grounded in true change can emerge, and from it just peace, when we as Christians and US citizens engage our leaders and call on them to implement a peace rooted in justice and respect for the aspirations of both peoples.

This Jerusalem Palestinian family, like Palestinians in the West Bank and Gaza, has experienced worsening conditions during the years of the "peace process." In negotiations, Israel has historically demanded "compromises" and concessions that merely cement past injustices—territorial loss, loss of sovereignty, and denial of the rights of refugees. Another precondition designed to codify Palestinians' inferior status has recently been added by the Netanyahu government—recognition of a "Jewish" state Palestinians know to be inherently discriminatory.

The Gospel mandate for peacemaking

THERE CAN BE no stronger mandate for peacemaking than the sermon on the mount in which Jesus promises that peacemakers shall be called children of God (Matt. 5:9). The United Presbyterian Church (U.S.A.) gave life to this mandate in 1980 when the General Assembly adopted the groundbreaking confessional

document, *Peacemaking: The Believers' Calling*. In it the church proclaimed (p. 17):

"God wills peace, 'shalom': total well-being, wholeness, fulfillment, health, joyous harmony... Peacemaking involves the utilization of political processes for social healing more than merely the assignment of political priorities. The biblical grounding of these truths is very extensive [citing Psalm 85:8,10, Psalm 37:11, Isaiah 54:10-17, Zechariah 8:12, Colossians 1:1-19, James 3:16ff]...."

Swords into plowshares

Additionally (p. 19), "The classical biblical image for peacemaking is the turning of swords into plowshares as found in the words of Isaiah 2:4: 'God shall judge between the nations, and shall decide for many peoples; and they shall beat their swords into plowshares, and their spears into pruning hooks; nation shall not lift up sword against nation, neither shall they learn war anymore.' Faith, hope, and love enable believers to give plowmak-

ing priority over swordmaking, not because such a strategy is more 'successful' but because believers are called to be peacemakers in the presence of enemies."

Peacemaking: The Believers' Calling has been endorsed by over 4,500 PC(USA) congregations over the past quarter century. It finds its grounding within the biblical and theological framework of an ongoing tradition of Presbyterian peacemaking.

A historic commitment to peacemaking

Even before 1980 a succession of General Assembly statements highlight the church's historic and consistent commitment to international peacemaking, beginning with a call in 1946 for the immediate cessation of the manufacture of atomic bombs. Other Assemblies issued statements in 1954, 1956, and 1962.

In 1969 the Assembly proclaimed that God is the Lord of conscience, not only of a participant in war for moral reasons, or the objector to all war on pacifist grounds, but also of those who conclude that a particular conflict is morally unconscionable.

And in 1970 it urged that in the absence of a declaration of a state of war...all military combat by the United States armed forces in Southeast Asia be terminated.

The 187th General Assembly in 1975 affirmed that the maintenance of economic advantages to sustain a high standard of living is not and cannot be considered just cause for supporting or participating in war or military action on the grounds that such action is inconsistent with the life and teaching of Jesus and the faith of the church.

In adopting *The Believers' Calling* in 1980 the 192nd General Assembly affirmed peacemaking and declared: 1) The church is faithful to Christ when it is engaged in peacemaking; 2) The

A delegation of 22 people from San Francisco Bay Area Presbyterian churches worked in February 2008 with the family of Izzat Abu Latifeh, a Palestinian olive farmer whose fields are located near Jaba'a in the Bethlehem Governorate, West Bank. Here, a "bucket brigade" of delegation members unloads a truck carrying olive tree seedlings while others prepare the ground for planting.

Solidarity delegations give Americans direct experience with Palestinian life under occupation and personal encounters with Israeli and Palestinian peacemakers. On Harvest Delegations, participants assist and accompany Palestinian farming families who often face harrassment and violence from Israeli settlers attempting to disrupt the annual olive harvest. During this Planting Delegation in February 2008, Palestinian olive farmer Izzat Abu Latifeh explains to Carl Basore of the Redwoods Presbytery how to plant a two-year-old olive tree seedling in rocky soil. In one day, delegation participants planted over 300 olive trees.

church is obedient to Christ when it nurtures and equips God's people as peacemakers; 3) The church bears witness to Christ when it nourishes the moral life of the nation for the sake of peace in the world (see www.pcusa.org/peacemaking/believers.pdf).

A reconciling vision of love through nonviolence

Eight years later, the Assembly stated, "Though the Reformed tradition has justified the resort to violence in response to particular forms of oppression, its emphasis on the reconciling vision of love presumes that the choice of nonviolence is more appropriate.

As a way of life…it seeks peacefully to affirm creation, to respect the value and dignity of all human beings, and to recognize the potential for human fulfillment in all of God's people."

Security through justice

In 1994 the General Assembly advocated:

• The development of regional and global institutions that transcend the divisiveness of national structures and are capable of coping with global problems of war, peace, and conflict resolution, and that can address economic, social, and environmental problems that cut across nation-state boundaries in an interdependent world.

• The development of a new meaning of security based on common interest, cooperation, and trust, understanding that if any country is to be secure, all must be secure, and understanding that military power can never be the ultimate basis for world security.

The invasion of Iraq

And in 2004: From the beginning, it has been the judgment of many church leaders, both in the United States and elsewhere, that an invasion of Iraq has been unwise, immoral, and illegal. The 216th General Assembly concurs with this judgment (see www.pcusa.org/acswp/pdf/iraq-resolution.pdf).

A Church Mandate for Palestine and Israel

At the meeting of the PC(USA) 218th General Assembly in 2008, a resolution was passed entitled "On Peace and Justice in Palestine and Israel." In the resolution, the church:

• Affirms the obligation of the church to speak to the governments of the United States and all other nations where it sees those governments violating the commandments of God;

• Endorses the "Amman Call" including its affirmation of the UN resolutions that are the basis of a projected "two-state" solution, a shared Jerusalem, and the human rights of refugees and occupied peoples;

• Commends the nonviolent witness of the Christians in Palestine and Israel;

• Encourages Presbyterian individuals, congregations, and councils to take pilgrimages and trips to Israel and Palestine that are in harmony with our principles [and] opportunities to meet Israeli and Palestinian peacemakers and to engage in interfaith discussion of a range of perspectives.

(Read full text of Resolution 11-01 at www.pc-biz.org)

> God's call to peacemaking is absolute. God is not a god of destruction, abandonment or death, but of life, peace, and joy, who is jealous for a dynamic and full response from Christians who are called to be peacemakers in a warring world. Faith, hope, and love enables believers to give plowmaking priority over swordmaking, not because such a strategy is more "successful" but because believers are called to be peacemakers in the presence of enemies.
>
> —*Peacemaking: The Believers' Calling* (pp. 17 and 19), based on Psalm 34:14, Hebrews 10:30ff, Ephesians 2:14-17

Part One: Perspective

CONFLICTING NARRATIVES

5 A Jewish narrative: evolving attitudes

7 A Palestinian narrative: then and now

9 Remembering the Nakba

SHAPING OUR UNDERSTANDING

12 Christian attitudes toward Israel

15 The American conversation

> I have spent a great deal of my life during the past 35 years advocating the rights of the Palestinian people to national self-determination, but I have always tried to do that with full attention paid to the reality of the Jewish people and what they suffered by way of persecution and genocide. The paramount thing is that the struggle for equality in Palestine/Israel should be directed toward a humane goal, that is, co-existence, and not further suppression and denial.
>
> —Edward Said, "Worldly Humanism v. the Empire-builders," *CounterPunch* August 4, 2003

Only a stone wall remains, marking the site of the Palestinian village Khirbat al-Duhayriyya in Khirbat district northeast of Al-Ramla. The village was attacked on July 10, 1948 by the Givati Brigade as part of Operation Dani. Israeli historian Benny Morris notes that the expulsion of the Palestinian residents of the Lydda-Ramla region in 1948 accounted for a full one-tenth of the Arab exodus from Palestine.

Noga Kadman

Six decades after the establishment of the state of Israel, there is growing awareness of the impact of that event on the Palestinian people. Broad recognition of the tragic history of Jewish persecution culminating in the Holocaust has been followed, if belatedly, by recognition of the price paid by the Palestinian people for European anti-semitism and Hitler's genocidal policies.

Even now, however, Americans are broadly familiar with the dominant Jewish narrative about Israel, but relatively few fully comprehend the Palestinian historical narrative and the ongoing story of their ethnic cleansing. This widespread imbalance in understanding is, itself, a barrier to peace. In his book *The Ethnic Cleansing of Palestine*, Israeli historian Ilan Pappe observes that retrieving the Palestinian story is "the very first step we must take if we ever want reconciliation to have a chance, and peace to take root, in the torn lands of Palestine and Israel."

Those who genuinely support the rights of both Arabs and Jews in the Middle East to live in peace must recognize the interdependence of the two peoples in their pursuit of human rights, security, and peaceful coexistence as equals. It does not diminish the importance of the Jewish narrative on Israel to advocate an equivalent awareness of the Palestinian experience both past and present.

A Jewish narrative: evolving attitudes

BY MARK BRAVERMAN

ZIONISM WAS the answer to the anti-Semitism of Christian Europe. The failure, despite the Enlightenment, to establish Jews as an emancipated, accepted group in Europe in the 18th and 19th centuries, and the rise of political anti-Semitism in the late 19th century gave birth to political Zionism under the leadership of Theodore Herzl.

Zionism expressed the powerful drive of the Jewish people to establish themselves as a nation among other nations, with a land of their own in which to achieve self-determination. The story of Jewish survival despite constant persecution at the hands of their oppressors is deeply embedded in the cultural DNA of the Jewish people.

Modern political Zionism springs from the Jewish experience over two thousand years of Jewish history; this experience colors the culture and the policies of the modern state of Israel. Although Zionism was a secular ideology, a religious version flourished after statehood, in which this reclamation of power was linked to a messianically-tinged belief in the fulfillment of God's promise to Abraham in the Biblical covenant.

In the dominant Jewish narrative about the birth of the State of Israel—a story until recently almost universally accepted throughout the Western world—the story of Israel's birth recapitulates Jewish history. In this story, the armies of the Jews' enemies had massed to destroy them time and again throughout history. But the founding of Israel changed history: the Jewish people fought back, defended themselves, prevented the disaster, and triumphed over their foes.

The Nazi Holocaust plays a dominant role in modern Israeli culture. The State of Israel is proof that in spite of the most extreme and systematic effort to destroy the Jewish people, they survived. Though this formulation of the relationship between the Nazi Holocaust and Zionism is commonplace, the historical reality is more complicated.

The stunning Israeli victory in the 1967 "Six-Day War," in which Israel conquered the Sinai, the West Bank, and Syria's Golan Heights, created a sense of euphoria in Israel and

Above left: "The Jews Who Will It Will Have Their State" (Zeev Raban, 1947) Theodore Herzl, after witnessing French mobs shouting "Death to the Jews" during the Dreyfus Affair, resolved that there was only one solution to Europe's persistent anti-Semitism: the mass migration of Jews to a land that they could call their own. Within a few years, Herzl had inaugurated the Zionist project with the goal of establishing a Jewish state in Palestine.

Above center and right: Zionist literature and graphic art, pre- and post-statehood, promoted images of tan, athletic men and women. The Jew, for millennia seen as servile, helpless, and excluded from the power structure, is now strong, self-determined, no longer a victim, and tied heroically to the land.

throughout the Jewish world. Israel's ambassador to the UN, Abba Eban, delivered a stirring address at the conclusion of that conflict, emphasizing and reinforcing the image of the tiny, beleaguered David of Israel vanquishing the Goliath of the armies of five Arab nations arrayed against it. The Biblical and messianic overtones of Israel's victory became predominant in Israeli culture. This feeling is seen as driving the activity to settle the occupied territories with Jewish Israelis, a process that has accelerated throughout the 60-plus years since 1948.

The power and persistence of the dominant Jewish narrative has had and continues to exert a powerful influence in the political sphere. A prime example is the belief that Israel has no partner for peace. Many, if not most, Israelis as well as diaspora Jews believe that there is "no choice" but to fight—that talking, sharing, and compromise will lead to disaster. The episodic outbreak of violence on the part of Palestinians and the growth of Palestinian political parties that accept violence as a legitimate form of resis-

Safe haven: ingathering of the exiles

Immediately upon establishing the state in 1948, Israel opened its borders to Jewish refugees from around the world. Holocaust survivors streamed in from displaced persons camps from across Europe. Israel's stated purpose is to provide a haven for Jews to live in security and to be a center for the development of a vibrant Jewish culture.

> "We [Israelis] do not distinguish between levels of hostility nor do we view our enemies as rivals with possibly legitimate needs; they are all against us all the time, and all we can do is defend ourselves.

—Avraham Burg, former speaker of the Israeli Knesset and author, *The Holocaust is Over; We Must Rise from Its Ashes*

tance to occupation has lent support to that belief. Many Jews hold the view expressed in this often-repeated statement: "If the Arabs were to put down their arms, there would be peace in a minute. If Israel were to lay down its arms, there would be a bloodbath, a second Holocaust."

I N AMERICA TODAY there is a range of Jewish attitudes toward Israel. The first is the "pragmatic" approach, which can also be called the appeal to "enlightened self-interest." "The Occupation," so this position goes, "is bad for Israel. Denying self-determination for Palestinians and subjecting them to the humiliation of a military administration breeds hatred and desperation, which is then visited upon Israelis in the form of violence."

Some American Jewish organizations who are opposed to the occupation but concerned that by voicing these concerns they will be labeled "Pro-Palestinian" adopt this position. "Israel," they say, "should smarten up and change its policies if it wants to live in peace and limit the economic drain of unending conflict." In informal conversations with some Jewish Americans who articulate

this position, they may confess that their position is really more strongly negative about Israeli policy, but that they feel it important to hew to this line for strategic purposes, in order to maintain credibility with the Jewish establishment as well as with government legislators in today's "pro-Israel" climate in the US.

Some Jewish progressives are more willing to speak directly to human rights and justice issues, while still holding on to a Zionist position. These voices acknowledge the issue of justice, but attempt to do this within the context of Jewish mainstream assumptions of entitlement with respect to the rights of the Jews to historic Palestine. This viewpoint limits the discourse to "the Occupation" and Israeli actions since 1967. It minimizes, avoids, or even denies the now well-documented history of the expulsion of three quarters of a million Palestinians from their cities and villages between 1947 and 1949.

Jewish critics of this position point out that avoiding the issue of the dispossession of the Palestinians fails to validate the experience of the other and maintains a position of Jewish ascendancy. Finally, it avoids the fundamental question, which is how a Jewish State, founded as a haven and a homeland for Jews, can provide justice and fair treatment for its non-

Jewish citizenry. It avoids the related and equally fundamental question of demography—the issue that, above all others, drives Israeli foreign policy and fuels the current political and military conflict.

Dr. Mark Braverman, a clinical psychologist and organizational consultant, is executive director of holylandpeace.org and serves on the advisory board of Friends of Sabeel North America. He is the author of *Fatal Embrace: Christians, Jews and the Search for Peace in the Holy Land*. Since 2006 he has devoted his full-time attention to Israel-Palestine peacemaking.

On the whole, Jews outside of Israel across a wide spectrum from "establishment" to "progressive," until recently have preferred to keep these questions off limits. Increasingly, however, Jews inside and outside of Israel have begun to ask how Israel can become the true democracy it proclaims itself to be in its Declaration of Independence—a country for all its citizens. What, these Jews are asking, can it mean to be truly "pro-Israel?" What would it mean to have an Israel committed, not to higher walls, but to opening Israel's vibrant culture to cooperation and exchange with the Arab world in which it lives? Indeed, Israelis and Jews around the world, along with Christians who want the best for the Jewish people, are seeing that the future for Israel lies in its opening itself up to coexistence with the Palestinian people with whom it shares the land, rather than further isolating itself behind walls of concrete and military power.

Jewish activists in San Francisco (above) and Seattle (right) are part of a fast-growing movement among American Jews who are asking important questions about what it means to be "pro-Israel." In the process, these Jews are challenging the mainstream establishment institutions that claim to speak for the entire community.

Cecilie Surasky

A Jewish Voice for Peace

"The whole world depends on justice."

Jewish Voice for Peace
www.jewishvoiceforpeace.org
Israelis and Palestinians. Two peoples. One future.

As a Jew I cannot support the Bombing of Civil...

As a Jew I cannot support attacks on

Joanna Kent Katz

The past two decades have seen stea growth in support for Jewish organizati that challenge the dominant mainstrea narrative on Zionism and Israel. Recog ing that the two peoples are destined tc share the land, many Jews recognize tha the aspirations of Palestinians and Israe are inextricably linked and that Jewish lit in Israel/Palestine cannot flourish withou respecting the human rights of Palestinia

A Palestinian narrative: then and now

BY NADIA HIJAB

WHEN ASKED TO describe what their cause is all about, most Palestinians will begin with the Balfour Declaration of November 2, 1917, when Britain promised the still small Zionist movement a "national home" in Palestine. Some will go farther back to 1897 and the Basel conference, where Zionism was born.

Palestinians start in the past because they have lived the history of their dispossession every day since 1917. And they can never forget the original sin, the flagrant injustice of an imperial power promising their country to another people. The Palestinians always ask: Why should we pay for what the Europeans did to the Jews? In 1917 the number of Arabs in Palestine—Muslims, Christians, and Jews—was about 650,000. A few thousand Zionist Jews had emigrated to Palestine since the end of the 19th century.

The Palestinians resisted British rule and plans for their country. They have always seen Israel as both a result and a continuation of 19th century colonialism. And, indeed, Israel's colonization continues to this day through the settlements it is building in the Palestinian territories occupied in 1967.

My mother's family left their home and their lands on April 28, 1948, seeking shelter in Syria from the clashes in Palestine and planning to return when quiet was restored. A few days earlier, on April 9, two terrorist Jewish groups (whose leaders both later became Israeli prime ministers) had massacred Palestinians at Deir Yassin and a Zionist whispering campaign

A Palestinian Arab family gathers hastily-packed boxes, bundles, chickens, and ducks on the dock in Haifa, Palestine, April 1948. Thousands of Palestinians from Haifa fled the advancing Zionist army and were evacuated on British military ships. As refugees, they believed they were leaving their lives, homes, and possessions temporarily; they were never permitted to return, and what they left behind was appropriated by Zionist statebuilders.

LIFE Magazine | palestineremembered.com

urged Palestinians to flee, to "remember Deir Yassin." My grandmother, a widow, had eight children; she and her four grown children got jobs to sustain the younger ones.

As a result of the creation of Israel in 1948, over 750,000 Palestinians fled or were forced to flee. They were never allowed back to their land and homes, in violation of international law. Palestinians struggled to survive their dispossession. The majority hailed from farms and villages and lived in refugee camps in Jordan, Lebanon, Syria, and Egypt, where millions live to this day. The ones with education found work and re-settled in Arab countries and around the world.

Richard Schlobohm

Nadia Hijab is a senior fellow at the Institute for Palestine Studies, an author, and a development consultant to international organizations. She co-founded the US Campaign to End the Israeli Occupation and serves on its advisory board.

The Palestinians who stayed on their land began the life of Arabs in a Jewish state. Although they were granted citizenship, they lived under Israeli military orders between 1949 and 1966—including curfews, detentions, and expulsions. The 1.5 million Palestinians now in Israel experience inequality and discrimination.

It is sometimes hard for people to understand the Palestinian attachment to their homes and their land. It is partly because this was an agricultural society rooted in the soil. But it is also because our society and country are so much part of how we Palestinians define ourselves. Being homeless means being rootless, living without a sense of belonging, always exposed to threat.

Perhaps the hardest part of the Palestinian struggle was to counter the myths the Zionist movement had spread to justify taking the land. One

Above: The author's grandparents with their first five children; three more would follow by 1945. The author's mother, Abla, is at far right. The Nashif family fled Palestine in 1948, settling as exiles in Syria; from there, descendants have become part of the Palestinian global diaspora.

In pre-1948 Palestine, the Nashif family earned a comfortable livelihood from agriculture and shopkeeping. The author's grandmother carried all the family's land deeds with her when she left Palestine, taking the box with her from country to country—but she died without ever going back home. The deed below shows family ownership of land around the village (now town) of Taybeh; the family also lost land between Taybeh and the Mediterranean Sea in 1948.

such myth was a "land without a people for a people without a land." But Palestine was settled and had been for millennia one of the oldest continuously inhabited parts of the world.

Another Zionist myth was "making the desert bloom." In reality, the Palestinians were such good farmers of the country known in Biblical times as "the land of milk and honey" that in the late 1800s a US consul wrote back home and said Florida orange producers could learn from the Palestinian farmers' techniques.

Even though the Palestinians have dreamed of turning the clock back to 1917, the earliest PLO political programs recognized that the Jewish community in Palestine was there to stay. In the 1960s, the PLO advocated a secular, democratic state in all of Palestine for Muslims, Christians, and Jews.

> "My grandmother always said the Palestinians never had a problem with the Jews as people. When her father would take her with him from Taibeh to Jaffa on one of his trips to market their produce, "We would share a meal with a Jewish family and spend the night with a Christian family."

The second PLO program, developed by 1974, was for two states living side by side, Israel constituting 78% of the country and Palestine the remaining 22% (lands occupied by Israel in the 1967 war). This has since been the basis of many peace plans—none implemented.

PALESTINIANS NO LONGER believe that Israel wants peace or that it will recognize that they have rights in Palestine. If Israel does want peace, then why has the number of Israeli settlers doubled since 1993 to some 500,000 today?

Israel always expresses fears about its security, but how does the colonization of Palestinian land contribute to Israel's security? On the contrary, the violence of the occupation, the endless injustice, and the hopelessness of life without rights have escalated the violence. The first suicide bombing against Israel took place in 1994, after 27 years of Israeli occupation.

Besides, Israel is one of the strongest states in the world, in military terms, and is a nuclear power believed to have between 200 and 400 warheads.

Oppressed people will always resist injustice. Most Palestinian resistance is nonviolent, but that fact rarely makes it into the American media. The first Palestinian uprising against the Israeli occupation in late 1987 was an almost completely nonviolent movement by civil society.

More recently, given the failure of the peace process and the weakness of the PLO, Palestinian civil society has taken the lead in advancing nonviolent strategies to bring an end to Israel's occupation. All who believe in justice are called to support boycott, divestment, and sanctions (BDS) against Israel until it upholds international law.

For Palestinians, a major source of hope is that many Jews, in Israel and around the world, are active in campaigning for Palestinian human rights. The involvement of Jews is an important expression of solidarity that greatly contributes to future peace among Palestinians and Jews.

Remembering the Nakba

> "It must be clear that there is no room for both peoples in this country.... this will not bring about the State of Israel....and there is no way besides transferring the Arabs from here to neighboring countries.

—Joseph Weitz, director of the Jewish National Land Fund, 1940, from *My Diary and Letters to the Children*, vol. II

O N MAY 15, 1948, the British Mandate of Palestine ended and Israel became an independent state. Contrary to Israeli versions of the story, Palestinians did not voluntarily abandon their homes. 250,000 already had been forcibly removed by Jewish militias before that date; 500,000 more were evicted by the Israeli military between May 15, 1948, and the Armistice of February 12, 1949.†

The United Nations adopted a plan to partition Palestine (Resolution 181) on November 29, 1947, in spite of the vigorous objections of Palestinian leaders and the Arab world. The partition plan allocated to Israel 54% of Mandate Palestine (containing over 400 Palestinian villages within its borders), although the Jewish population owned only 6% of the land at the time. Resolution 181 included no mechanism to keep the peace or prevent ethnic cleansing. Predictably, the indigenous Palestinians rejected any division of the land on which they had lived and farmed for centuries, particularly a division as inequitable as the one proposed. Palestinians protested with riots and looting, and Jewish forces retaliated. Ethnic cleansing began in December 1947 while British soldiers stood by and watched.

On March 10, 1948, (well before surrounding Arab nations joined the conflict), David Ben Gurion (who later became Israel's first prime minister) and his advisors implemented Plan Dalet, a military operation to depopulate and destroy Palestinian villages. The goal was the ethnic cleansing of Palestine's non-Jewish population. That night orders were sent to militia units providing detailed methods of destruction and listing the villages and urban neighborhoods to be "cleansed." In the months surrounding Israel's creation, Zionist forces committed at least 30 intentional massacres, killing thousands of unarmed Palestinians; 531 villages were destroyed; eleven urban neighborhoods were emptied of their inhabitants.

Mordechai Maklef (who later became the Israeli army Chief of Staff) ordered the Carmeli Brigade in Haifa to "kill any Arab you encounter; torch all inflammable objects and force doors open with explosives." Israeli historian Ilan Pappe describes the resulting exodus of Palestinians in his book *The

The United Nations answered the Palestinian refugee crisis in 1948 by establishing tent camps in Jordan, Syria, Lebanon, and the Palestinian areas controlled by Egypt (Gaza) and Jordan (the West Bank). Those camps, now densely packed concrete slums, have been home to registered refugees for more than 60 years. Today, the Palestinians displaced in 1948 and subsequent wars and their descendants number over seven million.

Ethnic Cleansing of Palestine: over 85,000 Palestinians living in Haifa and Jaffa were forced to exit their cities through the local seaports. Some tried to escape on small fishing boats while the Zionist militia attacked with rockets and guns. Overcrowded with their living cargo, many boats turned over and sank with all their passengers.

Six decades later, refugees await return, restitution

During the war in 1948, Zionist planners took measures to prevent Palestinians from returning to the homes they had left to escape the conflict. In August 1948 a "Transfer Committee" was charged with the destruction of depopulated Palestinian villages or their repopulation with Jewish immigrants newly arrived in Palestine. The Absentee Law, passed in December 1948, legalized the confiscation of vacant Palestinian properties. Prevented from returning home, some displaced Palestinians settled elsewhere in Palestine. Most were forced out of the

Noga Kadman

www.hanini.org

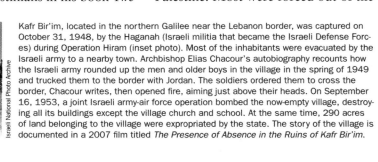

Israeli National Photo Archive

Kafr Bir'im, located in the northern Galilee near the Lebanon border, was captured on October 31, 1948, by the Haganah (Israeli militia that became the Israeli Defense Forces) during Operation Hiram (inset photo). Most of the inhabitants were evacuated by the Israeli army to a nearby town. Archbishop Elias Chacour's autobiography recounts how the Israeli army rounded up the men and older boys in the village in the spring of 1949 and trucked them to the border with Jordan. The soldiers ordered them to cross the border, Chacour writes, then opened fire, aiming just above their heads. On September 16, 1953, a joint Israeli army-air force operation bombed the now-empty village, destroying all its buildings except the village church and school. At the same time, 290 acres of land belonging to the village were expropriated by the state. The story of the village is documented in a 2007 film titled *The Presence of Absence in the Ruins of Kafr Bir'im*.

†Source: UNWRA

Zionism and ethnic cleansing: voices of Israeli leaders

"The Arabs will have to go, but one needs an opportune moment for making it happen, such as a war."

—David Ben-Gurion, Israel's founding father and first prime minister, 1937

"Neither Jewish ethics nor Jewish tradition can disqualify terrorism as a means of combat....First and foremost, terrorism is for us a part of the political battle...."

—Yitzhak Shamir, seventh prime minister, 1943

"Eretz Israel, [the 'Land of Israel,' including the West Bank and Gaza] will be restored to the people of Israel. All of it. And forever."

—Menachem Begin, sixth prime minister, 1954

"[Israel must] invent dangers, and to do this it must adopt the method of provocation-and-revenge...And above all—let us hope for a new war with the Arab countries, so that we may finally get rid of our troubles and acquire our space...."

—Moshe Sharett, second prime minister, before the 1967 War

"It is the duty of Israeli leaders to explain to public opinion clearly and courageously...[that] there is no Zionism, colonialization [sic], or Jewish State without the eviction of the Arabs and the expropriation of their lands."

—Ariel Sharon, Minister of Defense, then prime minister, 1998

"The ideology that enabled the depopulation of half of Palestine's native people in 1948 is still alive and continues to drive the inexorable, sometimes indiscernible, cleansing of those Palestinians who live there today.

—Israeli historian Ilan Pappe, 2006

borders of the newly-formed Jewish state altogether. Predictably, refugees attempted to return to their former homes; Israel treated them as criminal infiltrators.

UN Security Council Resolution 194 (December 11, 1948) stated that "refugees wishing to return to their homes should be permitted to do so at the earliest practicable date and that those choosing not to return should be compensated for their property." Israel's admission to the United Nations was conditioned on its compliance with this resolution. In the decades since, numerous resolutions have called for the return of Palestinain refugees and the end of Israel's occupation of the West Bank and Gaza. Israel has not complied: while using Resolutions 181 and 194 as legal support for its creation, Israel has rejected other resolutions as non-binding.

There is a growing campaign to deny the legal rights of Palestinians as a *quid pro quo* for losses experienced by Jewish refugees to Israel from Arab countries after 1948. Palestinian exiles, naturally, see it as yet another injustice that their legal rights would be canceled out by Middle Eastern Jews' property claims. Furthermore, Israel has actively promoted and subsidized Jewish emigration from Middle Eastern countries in its chronic struggle to build and maintain a Jewish majority.

Large numbers of the refugees ended up in the Gaza Strip. Approximately 80% of the 1.4 million people in Gaza, or about 850,000 people, are refugees and their descendants.

WITHIN ISRAEL'S borders, Palestinians face a different set of challenges as a result of their minority status in a self-defined Jewish state. Of the nearly one million Palestinians uprooted from their homes in 1948, some 150,000 remained within the boundaries of Israel. That population has grown

Map caption

Palestinian villages depopulated in 1948 and razed by Israel

Haifa · Sea of Galilee · Nazareth · Mediterranean Sea · Nablus · WEST BANK · Tel Aviv Jaffa · Jerusalem · Gaza · GAZA STRIP · Hebron · Dead Sea · Beersheba

Adapted from Palestinian Academic Society for the Study of International Affairs | www.passia.org

531 Palestinian villages were emptied and razed by Israel as a result of the 1948 conflict. Some of these villages' former inhabitants and their descendants have become part of the Palestinian diaspora. Others live within Israel today and experience discrimination as non-Jews living in a Jewish state.

The ongoing Nakba: Hebr[on]

In April 1968, less than a year after Israel's success in the Six-Day War, a few Israelis led by Rabbi Moshe Levinger rented a hotel room in the West Bank cit[y] of Hebron, ostensibly to celebrate Passover, then refused to leave, declaring the intention to create a permanent Jewish settlement there. Levinger's followers we[re] spearheading a movement to settle Jude[a] and Samaria, land they believed God had allotted to the Jews in the book of Deuteronomy.

Martha Reese

to nearly 1.5 million. Some live in villages that are "unrecognized" by the Israeli government and therefore receive no services such as electricity, running water, access roads, health and educational facilities, and sewage and communications services. Israeli laws have been drafted so as to legalize the Palestinian's dispossession and indeterminant status; the "present/absent" law, passed in the early 1950s, prohibits Palestinians expelled from their homes in 1948 from returning to them after having been "absent" for more than one month.

Lacking other alternatives, displaced Palestinians have rebuilt their homes and re-established villages—"illegally," according to Israeli law, but on land that was once theirs. Construction, including repairs to existing structures, is "illegal" and can be demolished at any time.

From the 1890s to the present, many Zionist leaders have dreamed of a "de-Arabized" Jewish state in all of "the Land of Israel." The Nazi Holocaust fueled international support for the Zionist idea that Jewish survival required a Jewish state. In the years since, maintaining a Jewish demographic majority in Palestine has brought expulsion, dispossession, and occupation to the indigenous Palestinian population—practices that continue to the present day in the West Bank, East Jerusalem, and Israel itself.

Palestinian refugees from Hawla and Tiberias in northern Palestine fled in 1948 to southern Lebanon and set up a tent camp near Tyre. The United Nations Relief and Works Agency started providing services in Burj el-Shemali camp in 1955; today the camp also houses displaced Palestine refugees from other parts of Lebanon. UNRWA has not been able to assist in rebuilding structures damaged during the 15-year Lebanese civil war because of a ban on entry of building material imposed by the Lebanese Government since 1998. The Lebanese government also imposes stringent restrictions on Palestinian refugees and their descendants living in Lebanon regarding employment and property ownership. As a result, unemployment is extremely high in Burj el-Shemali and other camps.

the presumed ancient burial site of [figu]res of major religious significance [to J]ews (as well as Muslims and Chris[tian]s), Hebron had an ancient, indigenous [Se]phardic Jewish community that lived in [rela]tive harmony with its Arab neighbors [unti]l the 1929 massacre of 67 Jews at the [han]ds of Arabs agitated by false rumors of [anti]-Muslim hostilities in Jerusalem.

Jewish settlers who followed in Rabbi [Le]vinger's steps after 1967 grew in num[ber;] they were also equipped with weap[ons] by the Israeli military and instructed [in t]heir use. Today four illegal Jewish [sett]lements are located within the city of Hebron, and others, including Kiryat Arba, surround the city. Approximately 10,000 Israelis inhabit the settlements in and near Hebron.

After February 1994, when settler Baruch Goldstein killed 29 Muslims inside Hebron's Ibrahim Mosque at the Tomb of the Patriarchs, Israel adopted a policy of separation between the settlers and Palestinians using a "security" strategy seen throughout the occupied territories: drastic movement restrictions and curfews imposed on Palestinians while Israeli settlers move freely.

A small number of today's Hebron Jews live in "reclaimed" properties, once owned by members of the ancient, indigenous Jewish community that lived in Hebron until 1929. Neither the settlers nor the Israeli government support a comparable restoration of Palestinian properties within Israel to their pre-1948 Arab owners.

B'Tselem, an Israeli human rights monitoring group reports that "hundreds of shops have closed, thousands of people have been left without a livelihood, and many hundreds of families have been forced to leave their homes. The city center has become a ghost town, where only Jews are allowed to move about freely."

Within the old city of Hebron, Jewish settlers number about 500 in a city of 130,000 Palestinians. They are protected by over 2,000 Israeli soldiers and an equal number of police. However, the soldiers have orders to protect only the settlers. Harrassment, vandalism, and attacks perpetrated by settlers against Palestinians occur almost daily. A senior official in the defense establishment has described Israel's policy as "a permanent process of dispossessing Arabs to increase the Jewish territory."†

Hebron is but one instance of how the simultaneous transfer of Jewish population into the occupied territories and dispossession of indigenous Palestinians are contributing to the project of maximizing the land area controlled by Israel while minimizing the number of Palestinians on that land.

†Amos Harel, "Report to Sharon and Ben Eliezer recommending enforcing the law on Hebron settlers," *Ha'aretz*, August 11, 2002.

Shuhada Street, once the center of a bustling commercial district in Hebron (*al-Khalil* in Arabic) are now empty, the shops welded shut by the Israeli military in 2000. Israeli settlers now refer to it as "the cleansed street." Nearly half of the Palestinian families living in central Hebron have been forced out, and 77% of their businesses have been closed.

Christian attitudes toward Israel

Holocaust theology and the "ecumenical deal"

THE HORRIFIC MAGNITUDE of the Nazi attempt to exterminate European Jewry was so profound that it took more than a decade to begin to articulate its meaning. After the 1961 trial of Adolph Eichmann and Israel's 1967 victory in the Six-Day war, Jewish theologians found their voice, producing a new genre called Holocaust Theology. Gradually, Christian theologians developed their own version of Holocaust theology, stressing the need for Christian repentance and a radical alteration of Christian theology. Two particular themes in Christian theology—deicide and supersessionism—were identified as having contributed to the persecution of Jews ever since the fourth century CE.

Deicide is the claim that all Jews are responsible for the crucifixion of Jesus. (See Matthew 27:25, "His blood be upon us and on our children!"; also Acts 5:28 & I Thes. 2:15-16.) Supersessionism is the claim that because Christians are heirs of the new covenant in Christ, the old covenant with Israel has been replaced; that salvation is through Christ alone. (See John 14:6...)

Many Christian Churches, recognizing the causal relationship between these Christian doctrines and anti-Semitism, have sought ways to repudiate theological tenets that foster contempt for Jews.

Unfortunately, Holocaust Theology has also had a negative consequence among Christians by stifling healthy exploration of the consequences of political Zionism.

Jewish theologian Mark Ellis calls this the Ecumenical Deal. "The deal began with the ecumenical dialogue between Jews and Christians after the Holocaust, when many Christians woke up and found there was blood on their theology," Ellis writes. "Israel became the vehicle for repentance for the Holocaust. Thus, for many Jews, any critical discussion of Israeli policy vis-à-vis the Palestinians is to abandon that vehicle of repentance and return to anti-Semitism. This is the ecumenical deal...." Ellis notes the dangerous result: "This ecumenical and political deal is killing Palestinians....First there was the crime against the Jews, and now there is the crime against the Palestinians."†

Organized segments of the American Jewish community have been vigilant in enforcing this "ecumenical deal," and Christian leaders and churches are often compliant when faced with orchestrated outrage or even the threat of it. Many incidents—intimidation, censorship, and self-censorship—occur behind the scenes and go unreported.

Difficult as it has been to foster open conversation on the Israeli-Palestinian conflict in American religious circles, there has been some progress, partly due to an opening of the discourse within the non-establishment Jewish community. In the last two decades, American Jews and Christians have begun to break the silence and move beyond the Ecumenical Deal. Increasingly, they are working together to support Israeli and Palestinian peacemakers, including Israelis who challenge their own country's oppressive policies toward the Palestinians.

American churches have found their voice. On 21 occasions since 1967, General Assemblies of the Presbyterian Church (U.S.A.) have broken the silence, calling for a just peace in line with United Nation resolutions. United Methodist, Episcopalian, Lutheran, UCC, and Disciples of Christ churches have issued similar demands. Churches for Middle East Peace includes 23 denominations and religious orders representing Protestant, Roman

Christians have been "native" to the Holy Land since the time of Christ, yet few Holy Land pilgrimages for Western Christians offer participants the opportunity to learn about these faithful communities of believers.

Donald Griggs

†Marc Ellis, "Is Peace Possible in the Middle East?" *Church & Society*, September/October 2003, pp. 78-79.

Bethlehem's inhabitants today are isolated and oppressed, surrounded by a 25-foot high concrete wall constructed by Israel. Jewish settlements are expanding on expropriated Palestinian land surrounding the city. Despite these dismal developments in the city of Christ's birth, there has been little outcry from concerned Christians around the world.

David Young

Catholic, and Orthodox churches engaged in the same quest for a just peace.

Biblical Israel and the modern political state of Israel

A PROBLEMATIC CONFLATION between the modern State of Israel and the biblical people of Israel has afflicted not only religious Zionists, but some Christians, too. Just as those opposed to ancient Israel were considered to be enemies of God, so are those who oppose policies and actions of the existing Israeli government. As a theological matter, this succeeds in making God a party to Israel's abuse of human rights in the occupied territories. It sacralizes the Israel-Palestine conflict in much the same way as do theocratic Islamists who preach holy war against Israel.

A study paper produced by the Presbyterian Church (U.S.A.) in 1987 entitled, "A Theological Understanding of the Relationship between Christians and Jews" affirmed that the geopolitical entity of the State of Israel is not to be validated theologically. A 2008 conference of the World Council of Churches on "The Promised Land" likewise concluded that "it is particularly important to differentiate between biblical history and biblical stories, and to distinguish between the Israel of the Bible and the modern State of Israel."

Christian theology: the Covenant and the Promised Land

Christian tradition provides at least four reasons to reject the State of Israel's claim to land based on biblical texts.

First, the tragic consequences which often come about when ancient religious texts are removed from their historical context and used to justify contemporary political ideologies and programs.

Second, the biblical requirement of obedience to God's way of justice and righteousness, which includes treating the stranger with kindness and hospitality, indeed as fellow citizens, as part of that same biblical Covenant (Deuteronomy 10:12-22).

Third, the New Testament teaching that Christians are part of that Covenant through God's son, Jesus, whose call is to reconcile all people, Jew and Gentile, into a peaceable realm in which stewardship of the land is required of all and the ethic of love of neighbor is the basis of "kingdom" citizenship (Romans 11:17; 14:17-18; Matthew 22:37-40).

And fourth, the long and seemingly intractable conflict between the modern State of Israel and the Palestinian people in which human suffering and human rights violations have stirred the Christian conscience.

The 2008 WCC conference referred to above emphasized, "[T]he Bible must not be utilized to justify oppression or supply simplistic commentary on contemporary events, thus sacralizing the conflict [between Israelis and Palestinians] and ignoring its socio-political, economic and historical dimensions." The WCC called on the churches to "critically and creatively examine notions of the 'Promised Land,' rediscovering in the Bible and in our traditions life-giving metaphors for promoting justice, peace, reconciliation and forgiveness for the fullness of the earth and all its inhabitants." Many eloquent speakers reiterated that in the contemporary world human rights and international law, rather than religious scriptures, must be the basis for national borders and behavior.

The genealogical claim to Israel

The founding narrative of the State of Israel links the modern-day Jews' claim to the land of Israel/Palestine to their direct genealogical descent from the ancient Israelites. Recent anthropological scholarship shows that this widespread belief is very likely a myth, not historical fact. Shlomo Sand, an expert on European history at the University of Tel Aviv, and author of *When and How Was the Jewish People Invented?* posits that the Jews were never exiled *en masse* from the Holy Land and that many European Jewish populations converted to the faith centuries later. Thus, he argues, many of today's Israelis who emigrated from Europe after World War II have little or no genealogical connection to the ancient land of Israel.

Because Jews, Christians, and Muslims all claim to be spiritual descendants of Abraham, theological claims to the land merely exacerbate the conflict by sacralizing it.

Christian Zionism's flawed theology

Christian Zionism is a predominately American movement that believes the modern state of Israel is the catalyst for the end of times, the fulfillment of biblical prophecy, and the return of Jesus with final judgment.

Christian Zionism has become a significant political force in the United

States. In an October 12, 2002 appearance on *60 Minutes*, televangelist Jerry Falwell said: "I think we can count on President Bush to do the right thing for Israel every time."

Televangelist John Hagee has recently developed a lobbying organization, Christians United for Israel (CUFI), which is well on its way to achieving its stated goal of having Christian Zionist offices and networks in every state of the union. CUFI fully supports the work of the American Israel Public Affairs Committee (AIPAC), the powerful pro-Israel lobbying organization.

CHRISTIAN ZIONISM is now, according to public polls, part of the American social/religious fabric with 59% of Americans believing the rapture will be an historical event (Gallup, 1999); 66% expecting Jesus' imminent return (National Opinion, 1996); and 46% believing that the state of Israel is the fulfillment of Biblical prophecy (National Opinion, 1996).

Hagee and other Christian Zionist leaders and organizations oppose the internationally accepted formula for a just peace between Israel and the Palestinians based on an independent and sovereign state of Israel alongside an independent, sovereign, and contiguous Palestinian state.

Christian Zionism elevates the

Core beliefs of Christian Zionism

The Covenant
God's covenant with Israel is eternal and unconditional; the promises of land given to Abraham will never be overturned. The church has not replaced Israel; therefore, Israel's privileges have never been revoked.

The Church
God's plan has always been for the redemption of Israel. When Israel failed to follow Jesus, the church was born as an afterthought or "parenthesis." At the rapture the church will be removed, and Israel will once again become God's primary agent in the world. We now live in "the times of the Gentiles," which will conclude soon. There are two covenants now at work, that given through Moses and the covenant of Christ. The new covenant in no way makes the older covenant obsolete.

Blessing modern Israel
Genesis 12:3 is applied literally and is applied to modern Israel: "I will bless those who bless you, and the one who curses you I will curse." Christians have a spiritual obligation to bless Israel and "pray for the peace of Jerusalem." While many Christians throughout history have also believed it important to observe the injunction of Genesis 12:3 in regard to the Jews, Christian Zionism links this specifically to support of the modern state of Israel. To fail to support Israel['s] political survival as a Jewish state will incur divine judgment.

Prophecy
The prophetic books of the Bible speci[fi]cally refer to events today, though som[e] may also refer to events in biblical times. Looking at Daniel 7, for instanc[e,] if we possess the right interpretative skills, we can see current events foreshadowed in it. This quest for prophec[y] has spawned countless books of endtime speculation (i.e., *The Late Great Planet Earth*, the *Left Behind* series, etc.) involving the state of Israel base[d] on biblical prophecy.

Modern Israel and eschatology
The modern state of Israel is a catalys[t] for the prophetic end-time countdown. [If] these are the last days, then we shou[ld] expect an unraveling of civilization, the rise of evil, the loss of international peace and equilibrium, a coming antichrist, and tests of faithfulness to Isra[el.] Above all, political alignments today w[ill] determine our position on the fateful day of Armageddon. Since the crisis o[f] 9/11 and the wars in Afghanistan and Iraq, it has been easy to persuade a large segment of the public that histo[ry] is unraveling precisely as dispensatio[n]ism predicted.

All these beliefs are rejected by the historic mainline Christian tradition.

rights of Israeli Jews while denying human and civil rights to Palestinians. It encourages Israeli policies that seek to drive Palestinians from their homeland and expand illegal Jewish settlements, and it supports the use of military force rather than diplomacy for resolving political differences between Israelis and Palestinians. Christian Zionism distorts Christian theology by omitting Jesus' command to love our enemies and seek peace based on justice.

Some Jews recognize the threat posed by Christian Zionism's brand of allegiance to Israel. Israeli journalist Gershom Gorenberg, in a *60 Minutes* interview on October 12, 2002, warns that "Christian Zionists do not see Jews as real people but as actors in their religious drama, where two-thirds of Jews are killed in one act, and the remainder must convert to Christianity."

John Hagee, televangelist and founder of Christians United for Israel, opposes any withdrawal by Israel from occupied territory. Addressing an AIPAC conference in March 2007, Hagee expressed concern that "in the coming months yet another attempt will be made to parcel out parts of Israel in a futile effort to appease Israel's enemies in the Middle East." But Hagee is confident in the power of his followers to shape the course of history. "The sleeping giant of Christian Zionism has awakened," he boasts. "There are 50 million Christians standing up and applauding the State of Israel."

The American conversation

Most Americans are fairly familiar with the dominant Jewish narrative about Israel, but relatively few know the Palestinian narrative and the ongoing story of their ethnic cleansing. One reason for this is the cultural familiarity with scriptures common to Judaism and Christianity. Another is the presence in the United States of a well-assimilated Jewish community that has built institutions with a capacity to engage with public opinion—and the relative immaturity of Palestinian advocacy institutions.

Skewed media coverage creates distorted perceptions

Another important factor in shaping public understanding is media coverage which has, historically, presented a skewed representation of the conflict. Bias in print and broadcast media typically manifests itself in several ways: word choice, e.g., the use of the term "by-pass roads" instead of "segregated roads"; placement, e.g., giving front-page coverage to Israel and burying a story about Palestine on the back page; lack of verification, e.g., accepting government "spin" as truth; selective reporting, as in maximal coverage of Israeli victims of Palestinian violence and minimal reporting on the victims of Israeli violence; decontextualization, as in reporting Hamas rocket attacks on Israel but failing to report the repeated assassinations and military incursions by Israel that provoke such attacks; coercion or censorship, like Israel's frequent denial of media access to the occupied territories and the targeting of reporters and photojournalists by Israeli tanks and snipers.

The most frequent form of bias is omission. Rarely does the mainstream US media report the daily violence of settlers against Palestinians or the ongoing nonviolent demonstrations by Palestinians against the construction of the Wall and the confiscation of their land. Rare, too, are stories that describe the overall impact of the occupation on both Palestinians and Israelis (though such coverage does appear in the Israeli media).

If the US media is overly dependent on official Israeli spokespersons, they are relatively deaf to the voices of Palestinians.

MARK REGEV
ISRAELI GOVERNMENT SPOKESMAN   CNN

US media are scrupulous about reporing the official Israeli version of events, which often describes acts of Israeli aggression as "responses" to Palestinian violence. Too seldom do media outlets include a Palestinian perspective on the Israeli actions that generate acts of Palestinian resistance, both violent and nonviolent.

Professors John Mearsheimer of the University of Chicago and Stephen Walt of Harvard University have published an analysis of the dynamics of what they call the "Israel Lobby" and its effects on public discourse in the US. "A key part of preserving positive public attitudes toward Israel is to ensure that the mainstream media's coverage of Israel and the Middle East consistently favors Israel and does not call US support into question in any way…" they write in their book *The Israel Lobby and U.S. Foreign Policy*. "[T]he American media's coverage of Israel tends to be strongly biased in Israel's favor, especially when compared with news coverage in other democracies." The chapter on "Dominating Public Discourse" describes the "objectionable tactics" used to create bias in the media, to promote one-sided analyses by think tanks, and to police the academic community.

Skewed coverage is no accident, writes Walter Rodgers, Jerusalem bureau chief for CNN from 1995 to 2000. "At the height of the second Palestinian intifada, Richard Griffiths, the editorial director of CNN, admonished me: 'You have to remember, Walt, there are two standards of reporting at CNN, one for Israel and the other for the rest of the world.' Like many in US news organizations responsible for Middle East coverage at that time, Griffiths had just taken a terrible beating from Jewish-American pressure groups as well as from his own avowedly pro-Israel management."†

Fortunately for those interested in peace, signs of change are on the horizon. Jewish Voice for Peace's Muzzlewatch Project is monitoring attempts to censor or slant media coverage and other forms of bias—a field that has, until recently, been dominated by multiple organizations monitoring the media for "anti-Israel" bias.

The changing tone of the debate

The last decade has produced groundbreaking writing that focuses on the key issues underlying the present situation. Much of this work takes direct aim at the myths, falsehoods, and denials that have been presented to the world at large and that help perpetuate the cycle of violence and political stalemate. Ilan Pappe, Avi Shlaim, and other Israeli "new historians" have published a side of the story that has, until recently, been absent from the public square. Increasingly, the American public is becoming aware that the obstacles to peace are complex and that Israel, far from being an innocent victim, bears major responsibility.

Former US President Jimmy Carter has reached many with his publication in late 2006 of a controversial book, *Palestine: Peace Not Apartheid*. In the book, he writes: "In order to perpetu-

†Walter Rodgers, *The Christian Century Magazine*, May 19, 2009, www.christiancentury.org/article.lasso?id=6941

ate the occupation, Israeli forces have deprived their unwilling subjects of basic human rights. No objective person could personally observe existing conditions in the West Bank and dispute these statements."

In published writing and speaking appearances, Archbishop Tutu of South Africa, who, like President Carter, compares Israel's policies in the occupied territories to South African apartheid, has called for a global social movement to oppose Israel's violation of human rights.

A GROWING CHORUS OF Israeli journalists and social critics expose the political and social damage inflicted on the state of Israel itself by the subjugation of Palestinians in the West Bank and Gaza; increasingly, Americans are listening to this important "other voice" on Israel.

In 2006 American-born Israeli historian Gershom Gorenberg published *The Accidental Empire: Israel and the Birth of the Settlements, 1967-1977*, showing how the power of the religious-settler movement and the failure of political will on the part of the Israeli government—including the "moderate" left-wing—has been responsible for continued conflict and the failure of successive peace initiatives. Avraham Burg, former speaker of the Israeli Knesset and former chairman of the Jewish Agency and World Zionist Organization, warns that Israel, "Holocaust-obsessed, militaristic, xenophobic, and, like Germany in the nineteen-thirties, vulnerable to an extremist minority," is in danger of losing its status as a democracy.

The internet has become an important alternative to corporate media for coverage of the conflict. Electronic Intifada is an influential, respected internet source of news and analysis from a Palestinian perspective.

Public awareness is also increasing

as the result of high-profile attempts to silence critics of Israel. Attacks on Jimmy Carter, Archbishop Desmond Tutu, and Professor Norman Finkelstein have exposed the tactics used to stifle open debate on US foreign policy in ways that myriad similar cases affecting lesser-known individuals have failed to do.

Jewish Voice For Peace and a number of other Jewish-led peace and justice organizations have been growing rapidly and gaining recognition in US (and other Western nations) over the past several years. The Washington, DC-based Campaign to End the Occupation is a coalition of over 260 local, regional, and national groups that oppose the Israeli occupation, advocate the application of international law, and challenge US policy toward Israel-Palestine. Last year, J Street, a new Jewish lobby in Washington, DC, was founded to counter the influence of the American Israel Public Affairs Committee (AIPAC) and "promote meaningful American leadership to end the Arab-Israeli and Palestinian-Israel conflicts peacefully and diplomatically." Also in 2008, the highly respected Israeli human rights monitoring organization B'Tselem

established an office in Washington, DC. Campus-based organizations such as Students for Justice in Palestine are proliferating on university campuses; Adalah–NY has implemented creative strategies including street theater for raising awareness.

Churches in the US are also showing an increasing willingness to challenge Israel's discrimination and dispossession of Palestinians. Disciples of Christ, Episcopalians, Lutherans, Methodists, Presbyterians, and the United Church of Christ are initiating educational, global mission, and advocacy projects, including initiatives to hold US companies accountable for their activities that contribute to and profit from Israel's military occupation of Palestine.

Many of those working to educate, inform, and mobilize are individuals who have traveled to Israel/Palestine for personal, direct experience with the conflict. Having heard from Palestinian and Israeli peacemakers challenging the status quo, these Americans return home with a powerful desire to share what they've learned. As more Americans are offered a balanced alternative to the Israel-centric perspective that has dominated during our lifetimes, it is to be hoped that there will be growing acceptance of the necessary conditions for a resolution of the conflict.

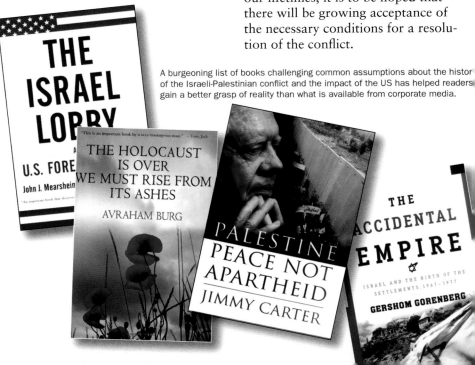

A burgeoning list of books challenging common assumptions about the history of the Israeli-Palestinian conflict and the impact of the US has helped readers gain a better grasp of reality than what is available from corporate media.

Part Two: Occupation

18 East Jerusalem
20 Settlements
22 Restricted movement
24 The Wall
26 Environmental occupation
28 War on Gaza
30 Resistance to occupation

> Israeli settlement expansion in Jerusalem and the West Bank continues apace. Peace would necessarily end Israel's land grab, while conflict and indeterminacy permit its continuation.
>
> —George Bisharat, "Has Israel's response exceeded its right to defend itself?" *San Francisco Chronicle*, January 5, 2009

1946
- Palestinian-owned land
- Jewish-owned land

1947 U.N. Plan
- Land designated for a Palestinian state
- Land designated for a Jewish state

1949–1967
- Palestinian land
- Jewish land (military and civil control)

2007
- Palestinian land
- Jewish land (military and civil control)

Map: original version by NAD-PLO; adapted from Oren Mediciks, 1999. Published in *Occupation Magazine*; modified by Engin Coban

2009

- Limited Palestinian sovereignty
- ▲ Jewish settlements beyond the Green Line
- Israeli military and civil control

Jenin

Tulkarm

Nablus

ELON MOREH

Qalqilya

ARIEL

MA'ALE EFRAM

SHILO

Ramallah

GIV'AT ZEEV

Jericho

MA'ALE ADUMIM

Jerusalem

BETAR

Bethlehem

EFRAT

SHIMA

Hebron

Map: www.passia.org

Following its victory in the Six-Day War of 1967, the government of Israel was divided about what to do with the territories newly conquered in battle. Some, including some of the Israeli government's legal advisors, made clear that keeping these territories and incorporating them into the state of Israel would contravene international law and international agreements which they had signed. The strong preference of the ruling Likud party, however, was to maintain control of the conquered land and annex it incrementally.

Decades of peace initiatives have yielded only relentless, incremental loss for the Palestinian people. While generations of Palestinians have been subjected to ever-diminishing levels of education, health, prosperity, and hope, the peace process has served as a smokescreen for Israel's annexation and settlement of Palestinian land and the confinement of the Palestinian people into ever-shrinking zones of isolation and deprivation.

Left: Rabbi Arik Ascherman, executive director of Rabbis for Human Rights–Israel was arrested at this 2008 protest against the demolition of a Palestinian home in the Jerusalem neighborhood of Silwan.

Right: Palestinian families watch helplessly as their homes and life savings are turned to rubble. Denial of building permits to Palestinians and demolition of Palestinian homes built without permits are two elements of Israel's discriminatory, quasi-legal system for obliterating the city's Arab and Muslim character.

Israeli Committtee Against House

EAST JERUSALEM HAS been militarily occupied territory since June 1967. The international community, including the United Nations and the United States, does not recognize the 1967 annexation of 70 sq. km of mostly vacant West Bank land to the municipal boundaries of West Jerusalem. The Geneva Convention prohibits unilateral annexation of territory acquired by military conquest.

On June 5, 1967, Israel initiated a preemptive strike by bombing and then invading Egypt, Jordan, and Syria with the goal of expanding the boundaries of the state. Six days later Israel controlled Gaza, Sinai, the Golan, and the West Bank along with both halves of Jerusalem. Almost at once the Israelis began reshaping the city by clearing a space along the western wall of the mosque compound known to Muslims as the Haram al Sharif and to Jews as the Temple

> Many of [Israel's] current illegal actions in and around the city have limited security justifications.... Israeli 'facts on the ground'—including new settlements, construction of the barrier, discriminatory housing policies, house demolitions, restrictive permit regime, and continued closure of Palestinian institutions—increase Jewish Israeli presence in East Jerusalem, weaken the Palestinian community in the city, impede Palestinian urban development, and separate East Jerusalem from the rest of the West Bank....
>
> —European Union Heads of Mission Report on East Jerusalem, December 15, 2008.

Mount. This operation involved the demolition of the 135 dwellings that constituted the Magharibah (Moroccan) quarter, along with a waqf (religious foundation) founded in the 12th century. All were bulldozed in one afternoon. The 1,000 residents of the quarter were scattered into the streets "at a few minutes notice." Another 5,500 Palestinians were driven out of the Jewish quarter.

On June 27, 1967, the Knesset passed legislation extending Israeli laws to East Jerusalem, resulting in annexation. The Israeli government expanded the municipal area of West Jerusalem by more than 70 sq. km to 108 sq. km. Israeli leaders announced that the process of integration was "irreversible and not negotiable."

The boundaries of the newly expanded municipality were gerrymandered to exclude Arab population centers, many of which were historically considered Jerusalem suburbs, and to include as much empty land as possible, particularly if it was prime agricultural land. On July 14, 1967, the UN General Assembly passed resolution 2254(ES-V) calling on Israel to rescind all measures already taken and desist from any further action that would alter the status of Jerusalem. This and other resolutions were simply ignored, with the backing of the United States.

Palestinians present at the time of the census following the 1967 War were granted "permanent resident" status, the same status as foreign citizens who are temporarily living in Israel, although these Palestinians were born in Jerusalem and had no

East Jerusalem

Theodore Settle

Har Homa was established by Israel in 1997 on Jebel Ghneim, occupied territory east of the Green Line. At the time, the US vetoed two different UN Security Council resolutions that called on Israel to stop its construction. Although Secretary of State Condoleezza Rice expressed official disapproval of Israel's 2008 expansion of Har Homa, no punitive measures have been suggested or imposed.

other home. Treating these Palestinians as foreigners who entered Israel is astonishing, since it was Israel that entered East Jerusalem in 1967. These "permanent residents" can vote in municipal elections, but are not allowed to vote for Knesset candidates, in contrast to Jewish citizens who moved into East Jerusalem after 1967.

Palestinian residents of East Jerusalem pay taxes, but receive few benefits. The municipality has failed to invest significantly in infrastructure and services (such as roads, sidewalks, water and sewage systems) in Jerusalem's Palestinian neighborhoods.

In 2003 Israel enacted a law that prohibits Palestinian residents of East Jerusalem or Israel proper from living with their spouses if the spouse is from the occupied territories. Since permits to travel to and from the occupied territories are hard to get, this law destroys family life.

Three generations of the Siam family became homeless in Silwan when their home was destroyed under Israeli decree. Between 1994 and 2006, 678 houses were demolished in East Jerusalem alone. From June 1967 to June 2009, over 24,000 homes have been demolished in the occupied territories. [Source: ICAHD]

Yotam Ronen | Activestills

While Palestinian communities in Jerusalem and environs are being choked and demolished, homes in Jewish-only settlements are being constructed, often on land expropriated from Palestinian owners. Large, high density settlement blocs visually dominate modern East Jerusalem.

Settlement construction has been continuous from 1967 to the present. By the end of 2001, 46,978 housing units had been built; not one of these was allocated for Palestinians, who constitute one-third of the city's population.

Since the Annapolis peace talks began in November 2007, nearly 5,500 new settlement housing units have been submitted for public review, with 3,000 so far approved, according to an EU Heads of Mission Report. There are now nearly half a million settlers in the occupied territories, including 190,000 in East Jerusalem.

Numerous settlements ringing East Jerusalem (including Har Homa, Gilo, Ramat Eshkol, East Talpiot, French Hill, and Malcha), are situated so as to irreversibly "Judaize" Jerusalem by creating facts on the ground that break up the Palestinian contiguity in Jerusalem and the West Bank.

Still more Palestinian land has been expropriated for the construction of ring roads and separation barriers that enable Jewish Israelis to move freely among settlements while paralyzing Palestinian movement.

Keren Manor | Activestills

Some of the land on which the Jewish settlement Nof Zion stands is owned by Palestinian families of the Jabal Al Mukhaber area of East Jerusalem. In 2005 the Palestinian owners of these tracts submitted an appeal to the Israeli High Court to prevent the building of Nof Zion, but the court rejected their petition. Nof Zion (Zion View) is one of 34 illegal settlements in East Jerusalem and the surrounding West Bank.

"The Israeli government and private Jewish groups are working in concert to build a human cordon around Jerusalem's Old City and its disputed holy sites, moving Jewish residents into Arab neighborhoods to consolidate their grip on strategic locations....The Israeli government has sometimes violated its own laws and regulations to advance the encircling effort....

—John Ward Anderson, *Israelis Act to Encircle East Jerusalem Enclaves in Arab Areas, Illegal Building Projects Seen Intended to Consolidate Control*, Washington Post, February 7, 2005

Settlements

ISRAELI SETTLEMENTS are colonies for inhabitation by Israeli Jews only, constructed in the Palestinian territories of East Jerusalem and the West Bank which Israel occupied after the Six-Day War in June 1967. The view among many Jewish Israelis in power at that time was that the Six-Day War had provided redemption for the Land of Israel (Eretz Israel).

Planning for the strategic placement of settlements in the West Bank began immediately after this war and has been an integral policy of each elected government since then. "There must not be the slightest doubt regarding our intention to hold the areas of Judea and Samaria for ever," wrote Mattiyahu Drobless, architect of one of the takeover plans. By locating settlements on prominent hills, Israel could control all the Palestinian aquifers while also dominating the horizon as a constant, intimidating reminder of the Israeli conquest.

Since 1967 Israel has seized more than 40 percent of West Bank lands,

This settlement, built on a hill near Nablus, shows both permanent housing and mobile caravans. Caravans are often the first phase of illegal settlement activity, followed by permanent housing, then roads and other infrastructure. From small, isolated beachheads, settlements typically encroach further onto surrounding land and grow in population. Settlers sometimes engage in harrassment and violence toward Palestinian landowners in the vicinity.

allocating them to settlements erected over the years. Now, nearly half a million Israelis live in the occupied territories: 285,000 in over 121 settlements and 100 outposts in the West Bank and 193,700 in settlements in and around East Jerusalem. Although the international community regards all these colonies as a breach of international law and UN resolutions, the Israeli government has authorized and subsidized the settlements and provides services to the outposts. US foreign assistance contributes to their construction and defense. Israeli Jews are provided financial incentives to participate in the colonization of Palestinian land.

Israeli settlement colonies are a major obstacle to peace because, in the words of President George Bush, "Swiss cheese isn't going to work when it comes to the outline of a state." The colonies and the infrastructure that links them to Israel imprison Palestinians into isolated

enclaves, eviscerate the Palestinian economy, and prevent the creation of a viable, contiguous, sovereign, and independent Palestinian state.

Many thousands of acres around settlements are closed to Palestinian entry. Settlers have placed physical obstructions far from the last houses of the settlement, patrol paths that they have built on Palestinian land, and expel Palestinians from this land. The state of Israel also contributes to this expropriation of Palestinian land by building by-pass roads and buffer zones to connect these settlement-colonies with Israel. These Israeli-only roads are off-limits to Palestinians who are cut-off from their schools, hospitals, markets, and extended families and friends.

Every Israeli government since 1967, whether led by Labor, Likud, or Kadima, has supported the colonization of more and more Palestinian land. In spite of promises made during peace talks beginning with Oslo in 1993, Israel has continued to create new settlements and expand existing ones. "What we're seeing is a classic example where a diplomatic

The Bush legacy

Publicly, the administration of George W. Bush opposed Israeli settlement construction. The Road Map of 2003, initiated by the US and backed by other members of the "Quartet" (US, UN, EU, and Russia), called on Israel to halt all construction in the settlements, including their "natural growth." At no point, however, did Israel stop settlement construction and expansion, including construction that Israel itself deems "illegal." US Secretary of State Rice issued periodic protests, calling settlement construction "not helpful" and "a problem," but no punitive measures were proposed, much less taken, against Israel for its noncompliance.

Israeli Prime Minister Netanyahu rejects Obama administration bans on settlement expansion, citing secret "agreements" and private "understandings" between his predecessor Ehud Olmert and the Bush administration that construction in existing Jewish settlements could continue as a quid pro quo for Israel's pull-out from Gaza in 2005.

> "While negotiations have been going on for 15 years, hundreds of thousands of Jewish settlers have moved in to occupy the West Bank. Palestinians say they can't have a state with Israeli settlers all over it, which the settlers say is precisely the idea.

— Bob Simon, CBS's *60 Minutes*, January 25, 2009

initiative has the effect of accelerating settlement construction," observed Gershom Gorenberg in June 2008. "When there is a fear or suspicion that a diplomatic process might actually take place, however unlikely that seems to outside observers, there is a tendency among settlement supporters within the government to try to speed things up."

Occasional attempts to uproot settlers are sensational media events, pitting fanatical religious-nationalist settlers against soldiers and police. These periodic demonstrations of government toughness have no effect in reducing the total settler population; removals of small encampments are portrayed as "painful concessions" that threaten the fabric of Israeli society—and the settlers often rebuild without interference outside the glare of media attention.

Riots ensued in December 2008

when settlers were forced to evacuate a building in Hebron they had occupied illegally. Prime Minister Ehud Olmert said, "Immediately after the evacuation, there were actions that cannot be described except as attempted pogroms by Jews from the Hebron area and other areas against Palestinian residents in Judea and Samaria. We are the children of a people whose historic ethos is built on the memory of pogroms....As a Jew, I am ashamed that Jews could do such

a thing."

In a less-visible way, the Israeli land-grab of the Jordan Valley is already complete. Virtually all of the land in the Jordan Valley, other than actual built-up areas of the Palestinian population, is under the control of the settlements' regional councils (and off-limits to the Palestinians). Almost all of the Jordan Valley settlements, despite having tiny populations, nonetheless have huge footprints on the land, with extensive agricultural areas.

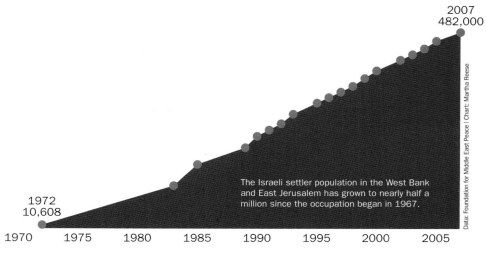

2007
482,000

1972
10,608

The Israeli settler population in the West Bank and East Jerusalem has grown to nearly half a million since the occupation began in 1967.

1970   1975   1980   1985   1990   1995   2000   2005

Data: Foundation for Middle East Peace | Chart: Martha Reese

Left: Although all settlements in occupied territory are illegal under international law, Israel defines as illegal only "outposts" built without state planning permission. Israeli security forces demolish settlement outposts periodically, as happened in May 2009 at Maoz Esther, this hilltop site northeast of Ramallah. Such outposts are often rebuilt immediately without government interference and, over time, may be declared legitimate.

Below An armed fundamentalist West Bank settler threatens a Palestinian farmer harvesting her olives, April 2005. Palestinian victims of settler violence receive virtually no protection by Israeli police and army personnel. Israeli and international solidarity activists have documented criiminal settler activity, like this encounter witnessed by the International Women's Peace Service. Still, settlers are very rarely charged or punished for criminal violence against Palestinians and their property.

IWPS

Oren Ziv / Activestills

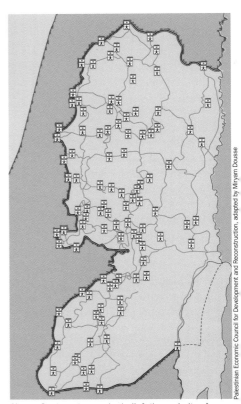

Left: Sophisticated "terminals" like the Al Qader checkpoint give an appearance of normalcy to Israel's regime of movement restrictions. The ring road system of which this checkpoint is part isolates Jerusalem from its West Bank terland, fulfilling Israeli policies first formulated in the 197 As a result of decades of settlement construction, there a now more Israelis than Palestinians living in the Bethleher Governate where the Gush Etzion settlement block is loca its two dozen Israeli settlements include Alon Shevut, Beit Illit, Efrata, Neve Daniel, and Tekoa. This zone is also a m source of Palestinian water resources expropriated by Isra

Palestinian Economic Council for Development and Reconstruction, adapted by Miryam Dousse

Israel has set up over 600 checkpoints, road-blocks, and segregated roads in the West Bank. The Israeli government claims checkpoints are necessary to prevent Palestinian attacks on Israelis, but checkpoints primarily restrict movement between Palestinian cities and villages, not between the Palestinian territories and Israel, at the same time preventing access to hospitals, schools, jobs, and farms.

Fixed checkpoints are permanent barriers manned by soldiers or police to restrict the free movement of pedestrians and vehicles, causing long delays. Abusive and humiliating confrontations often occur.

Random checkpoints (also known as "flying checkpoints") are temporary sites where the military and police stop pedestrians and vehicles to screen them for permits or to impede movement.

Roadblocks are concrete barriers, large stones, or high dirt piles that block the passage of vehicles on Palestinian roads. These barriers are usually unguarded and do not prevent people from crossing on foot, but they are a form of economic harassment because drivers are forced to transfer goods from a vehicle on one side of the roadblock to another on the other side. Instead of using their cars on the main road, Palestinians have to take indirect, unpaved roads or taxis that shuttle back and forth between road-

Above: Contrary to popular belief, the majority of checkpoints in the West Bank are not between the West Bank and Israel's internationally recognized borders, but rather within the Palestinian West Bank, most of them between Palestinian towns and villages.

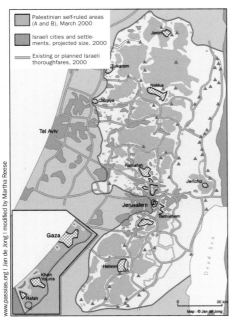

Palestinian self-ruled areas (A and B), March 2000

Israeli cities and settlements, projected size, 2000

Existing or planned Israeli thoroughfares, 2000

www.passia.org | Jan de Jong | modified by Martha Reese

Map: © Jan de Jong

A segregated network of roads built by Israel in the West Bank and linking it to Israel has consumed extensive tracts of Palestinian-owned land. These roads, while obscuring the border to Israelis, enable freedom of movement to settlers while inhibiting the movement of native Palestinians who are prohibited from using or crossing these roads.

essa lives in the village of Deir Ballut. At 2 a.m. one morning when Hessa was seven months pregnant with twins, she started having contractions. She and her husband hastily made their way to the checkpoint outside their village to get a ride to the nearest hospital in Ramallah, 25 miles away. But the Israeli soldiers would not allow them to pass because the checkpoint is open only from 7 a.m. to 7 p.m. "Look, we didn't make the rules, and we don't even agree with them. We're just following orders," the soldiers explained. Hessa's husband pleaded with the soldiers for over two hours before they agreed to telephone their superiors for an exception to the rule. Before the ambulance could get to her, Hessa had given birth to premature twins. One died on the way to the hospital, the other at the hospital.

Restricted Movement

blocks, making even short distances difficult or impossible to cover quickly and efficiently.

Bypass roads (called "Lateral Roads" in the Oslo agreements) link settlements with one another and with Israel, circumventing Palestinian built-up areas. These roads include a 50- to 75-meter-wide buffer zone, in which no construction or planting is allowed. In effect, these roads—often constructed on expropriated Palestinian land—carve up the West Bank into isolated ghettos and often deprive Palestinians of vital agricultural land and the income from it.

As of August 2008, 493 miles of bypass roads were in use. These roads are restricted to Israelis with yellow license plates on their cars. Palestinian vehicles, identified by green license plates, are not allowed on these roads without a permit. Permits are difficult or impossible to obtain and expensive. Palestinian tranportation is relegated to inferior secondary roads that are, themselves, restricted by checkpoints and roadblocks.

The Israeli policy of dividing Palestine into fragmented, isolated cantons is based on the assumption that Israel's security needs justify not only control of its border with the territories, but the disruption of Palestinian life beyond the Green Line. In order that Israeli settlers may live in security and move freely, Palestinians live with little security and face sweeping restrictions on movement, a flagrant violation of international law.

Territorial expansion in the guise of security control drives the design of Israel's system of roads and barriers in the West Bank. The Israeli government's Settlement Master Plan for 1983-86 states: "The road is the factor that motivates settlement…and [road] advancement will lead to development and demand." Clearly, easy vehicular access has been an attractive feature for settlers.

Instead of making Israel more secure, these policies undermine Israeli security by strengthening the Palestinian will to resist occupation and dispossession.

Above: An elderly Palestinian woman pleads with an Israeli soldier to let her cross the Ar-Ram checkpoint in January 2007. This incident, like hundreds of others, was photographically documented by the Israeli human rights organization Machsom Watch.

Below: A Machsom Watch member monitors the restriction on movement imposed by a cement-block barrier at the Kedar road in July 2005. For their work in documenting and sometimes intervening against abuses by the Israeli military at checkpoints, Machsom Watch's members—mostly Israeli women—have earned the respect of the Palestinians who seldom encounter sympathetic Israelis.

Left: Roadblocks like this one at Qarawat Bani Hassan in the Salfit region (see map on page 26) are set up and removed unpredictably, disrupting the transportation of Palestinian goods. The nearby village of Marda is served by three roads, but only one is open at any given time because of roadblocks. Palestinian goods are costly to transport since they must be carried by hand from truck to truck past roadblocks. As a result, Israeli products are often cheaper than their Palestinian counterparts, leaving captive-market Palestinian consumers a difficult choice between paying a premium for Palestinian products or subsidizing the occupier with their purchases.

The Wall

Mohammad Jalud lives in a village near Qalqilya on the east side of the wall. His fields are on the west side, just 10 minutes away, through a gate in the wall not open to Palestinians. After many applications he obtained a permit to enter a distant gate, but the trip to his fields then took one hour each way. Often he had to wait hours for the gate to be opened. Israeli officials refuse to allow him to take his tractor to his farm. He must carry all his farm implements and produce on his back, for even a donkey requires a permit. In 2005 he lost his entire crop because of these difficulties. If he takes a job and lets his land lie fallow, it will be confiscated under the Absentee Property Law.

IN JUNE 2002 the government of Israel began constructing a physical barrier to separate Israel and the West Bank. In most areas, the barrier is an electronic fence with sterile zones, barbed-wire fences, and trenches on both sides, consuming a strip of land averaging 196 feet in width. In populated areas, a concrete wall 20 to 26 feet high has been erected.

The land on which the barrier is built is is not within Israel or on the border (the Green Line); it is on Palestinian land that Israel has occupied since the 1967 war.

The barrier has brought untold

The 1,800 residents of 'Azzun 'Atmeh are imprisoned in an enclave created by the Separation Barrier. In 2007 a resident who was injured in an accident died after soldiers at the barrier gate refused to allow his evacuation to a hospital in Qalqiliya.

Miki Kratsman | *Ha'aretz*

hardships for hundreds of thousands of Palestinians. The suffering has been particularly acute for those who depend on agriculture for their livelihoods. The land between the Green Line and the barrier is called the "seam zone" and is one of the most fertile areas of the West Bank. Along this seam zone thousands of Palestinians on both sides of the barrier are being driven into poverty by restrictions on residency, lack of access to farm lands, inability to market their crops, and confiscation of land. A small percentage of landowners living on the eastern side of the barrier are granted permits to farm land they own on the western side of the barrier.

When finished, the wall/barrier will usurp an additional 11.9% of Palestinian land in the West Bank. The agricultural Jordan Valley area—about 30% of the West Bank—is already off limits to Palestinians and has undergone a de-facto annexation to Israel.

Israel points to the dramatic decline in the number of suicide bombings since 2002 as justification for the barrier. Israel's right to defend its inhabitants from violence is undisputed; however, collective punishment of an entire population for the violent actions of a few is illegal. Furthermore, the route of the barrier does not separate Israel from the Palestinian

David Young

territories but is situated to solidify the expropriation and annexation of Palestinian land for the construction and expansion of Jewish settlements which are, themselves, illegal.

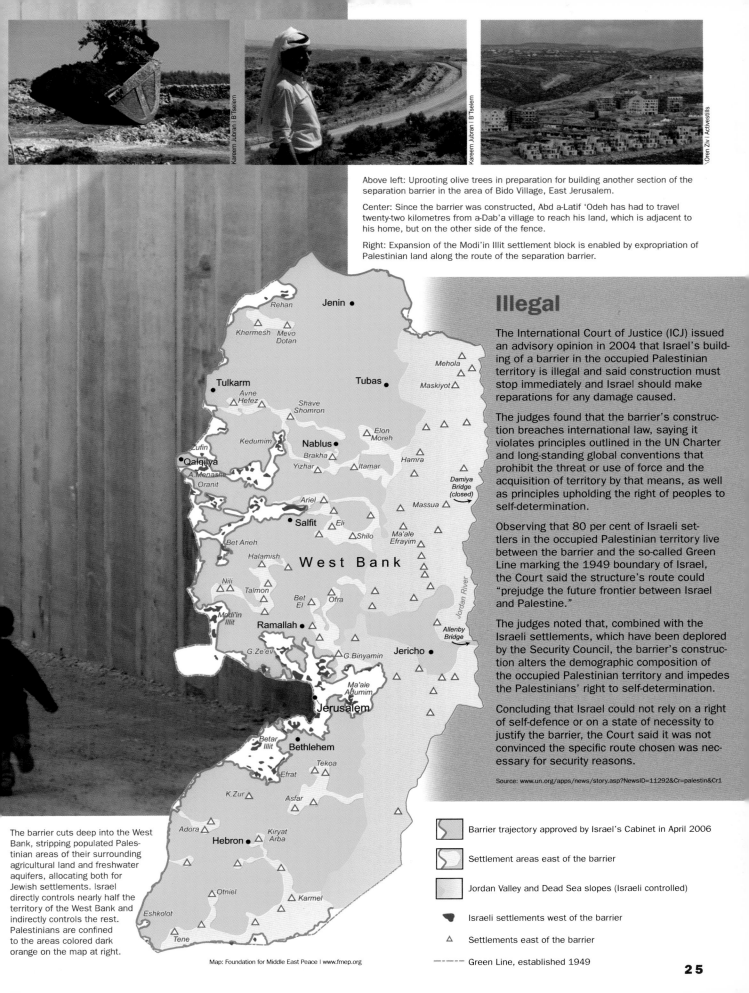

Above left: Uprooting olive trees in preparation for building another section of the separation barrier in the area of Bido Village, East Jerusalem.

Center: Since the barrier was constructed, Abd a-Latif 'Odeh has had to travel twenty-two kilometres from a-Dab'a village to reach his land, which is adjacent to his home, but on the other side of the fence.

Right: Expansion of the Modi'in Illit settlement block is enabled by expropriation of Palestinian land along the route of the separation barrier.

Illegal

The International Court of Justice (ICJ) issued an advisory opinion in 2004 that Israel's building of a barrier in the occupied Palestinian territory is illegal and said construction must stop immediately and Israel should make reparations for any damage caused.

The judges found that the barrier's construction breaches international law, saying it violates principles outlined in the UN Charter and long-standing global conventions that prohibit the threat or use of force and the acquisition of territory by that means, as well as principles upholding the right of peoples to self-determination.

Observing that 80 per cent of Israeli settlers in the occupied Palestinian territory live between the barrier and the so-called Green Line marking the 1949 boundary of Israel, the Court said the structure's route could "prejudge the future frontier between Israel and Palestine."

The judges noted that, combined with the Israeli settlements, which have been deplored by the Security Council, the barrier's construction alters the demographic composition of the occupied Palestinian territory and impedes the Palestinians' right to self-determination.

Concluding that Israel could not rely on a right of self-defence or on a state of necessity to justify the barrier, the Court said it was not convinced the specific route chosen was necessary for security reasons.

Source: www.un.org/apps/news/story.asp?NewsID=11292&Cr=palestin&Cr1

The barrier cuts deep into the West Bank, stripping populated Palestinian areas of their surrounding agricultural land and freshwater aquifers, allocating both for Jewish settlements. Israel directly controls nearly half the territory of the West Bank and indirectly controls the rest. Palestinians are confined to the areas colored dark orange on the map at right.

Map legend:

- Barrier trajectory approved by Israel's Cabinet in April 2006
- Settlement areas east of the barrier
- Jordan Valley and Dead Sea slopes (Israeli controlled)
- ● Israeli settlements west of the barrier
- △ Settlements east of the barrier
- - - - - Green Line, established 1949

Map: Foundation for Middle East Peace | www.fmep.org

Map labels: Jenin, Rehan, Khermesh, Mevo Dotan, Mehola, Maskiyot, Tulkarm, Tubas, Avne Hefez, Shave Shomron, Elon Moreh, Kedumim, Zufin, Nablus, Brakha, Hamra, Qalqilya, Yizhar, Itamar, A.Menashe, Oranit, Damiya Bridge (closed), Ariel, Massua, Salfit, Eli, Shilo, Ma'ale Efrayim, Bet Arieh, Halamish, West Bank, Nili, Talmon, Bet El, Ofra, Jordan River, Modi'in Illit, Ramallah, Allenby Bridge, G.Ze'ev, G.Binyamin, Jericho, Ma'ale Adumim, Jerusalem, Betar Illit, Bethlehem, Tekoa, Efrat, K.Zur, Asfar, Adora, Kiryat Arba, Hebron, Otniel, Karmel, Eshkolot, Tene

25

Anna Baltzer

Right: Israeli bulldozers arrived and began uprooting olive trees in the West Bank town of Kifil Haris (near Nablus) in December 2003. The army claimed to be expanding the settler road; other officials said they were excavating for a new water system; Haris' families feared the demolitions indicated that their village was on the planned route of the separation barrier. In the absence of official maps of the barrier's route, Palestinians find it difficult to mobilize resistance against demolitions.

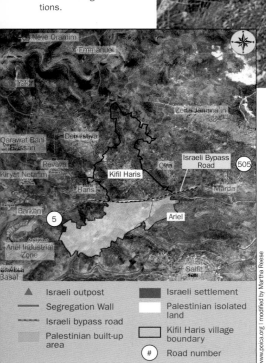

▲ Israeli outpost

— Segregation Wall

••• Israeli bypass road

  Palestinian built-up area

  Israeli settlement

  Palestinian isolated land

  Kifil Haris village boundary

  (#) Road number

www.poica.org | modified by Martha Reese

Above: Within a few years of the bulldozers' destroying Kifil Haris' olive trees, Israel's strategic objective had become apparent. Route 505, a new settler bypass road was constructed, splitting the village in two sections and isolating 1,100 acres of the village's lands. The separation barrier surrounding Ariel settlement bloc consolidates this expropriation. Already 133 acres of the village's lands have been confiscated and allocated to Ariel. See map at www.poica.org/editor/case_studies/KH_08.jpg.

Right: On October 11, 2008, the residents of Burin and nearby villages went to harvest olives in their fields, next to which the settlement of Yitzhar was established in 1984. While harvesting they were attacked by settlers who threw stones at the Palestinians and damaged their olive trees. There is a history of violence between villagers and the settlement's Orthodox Jewish residents, who currently number about 500. The settlement is located deep inside the occupied Palestinian territories near Nablus.

Environmental Occupation

As olive trees are uprooted, so are Palestinians' lives

A MILLION AND A quarter trees and thousands of acres of farmland have been destroyed in Palestinian territories by Israelis since 1967. Nearly 465,000 olive trees were uprooted between 2000 and 2005, and the destructive practices continue to the present time.

Destruction of agricultural tracts is perpetrated in two forms: Israeli military actions in support of state land expropriation and destructive vandalism by Jewish settlers.

Palestinians face draconian restrictions on the movement of people and goods in the territories. Many Palestinian farmers cannot reach their agricultural lands to tend and harvest their crops due to road closures. The separation barrier has deepened the agricultural crisis, permanently separating Palestinian families from

Yotam Ronen | Activestills

their farmlands, except for locked, unmanned gates that allow unpredictable access.

Under a law from the Ottoman era, Israel claims as state property land that has been "abandoned" and left uncultivated for four years. This land is then usually declared Israeli state land and often later allocated to Israeli settlements for expansion. By making it almost impossible for some farmers to get to their land, Israel can claim that Palestinian land has been "abandoned." Often, land expropriation is effected without resort to even such bureaucratic chicanery as this.

Olive trees are a major source of livelihood for many Palestinian

The occupation's manifest harm to the environment is pervasive and profound. Its effects encompass a broad spectrum of hazards from overextraction of groundwater, to the effect of the Wall on rainwater runoff and animal migration, to infrastructural restrictions on the Palestinians' own capacity for rubbish disposal, to the dumping of settlement rubbish and sewage on Palestinian agricultural land, as shown in this 2005 photo taken at Deir Sharaf.

families. By targeting olive trees, the Israeli government is sabotaging the Palestinian economy.

World Bank reports have condemned the uprooting of olive trees as violating the trade policies of the Paris protocols of 1954 which calls for "free access for Palestinian goods to the Israeli market and vice versa." Property destruction also violates Article 33 of the Fourth Geneva Convention, which prohibits collective punishment.

Israel's control of water supply leaves Palestinians thirsty

SINCE THE BEGINNING of the occupation in 1967, Israel's strict control of the water sector in the occupied territories has prevented development to meet Palestinian water needs, and caused shortages and a water-quality crisis.

Water in the occupied Palestinian territories has been fully incorporated into the Israeli water-management system to the general benefit of Israel and detriment of Palestinians. About 70% of groundwater on which Israel is dependent and 40% of its annual fresh water supply originate in the occupied territories. Of the water available from West Bank aquifers, Israel uses 73%, West Bank Palestinians use 17%, and illegal Jewish settlements use 10%. As a result, West Bank Palestinian water consumption is 40 liters per day less than the minimum global standards set by the World Health Organization (WHO).

Israel is in control of all water development in the West Bank. Israel can veto any Palestinian requests to drill wells or collect surface water. It is difficult if not impossible for Palestinians in occupied territories to get permission to drill a new water well or even repair one. Because of the water shortage, many Palestinians have to buy water from tankers; poor families

Gaza's water crisis is even more profound than that in the West Bank. The aquifer that provides 96% of water consumed in the Gaza Strip has become polluted and salinated due to over-extraction and penetration of untreated sewage and agricultural runoff. Only 7% of the water in the Gaza Strip meets WHO standards. The siege and blockade imposed by Israel since 2006 has made maintenance of infrastructure nearly impossible; the winter war of 2008-2009 shattered Gaza's already-failing water treatment and delivery capacity.

spend up to one-fifth of their income on water.

Israel has neglected construction of infrastructure to connect the Palestinian rural population to a running-water network as well as proper maintenance of existing networks. In 2008, 227,500 Palestinians in 220 towns and villages were not connected to a water network. Another 190,000 Palestinians are only partially served.

In the West Bank, about 50 groundwater wells and more than 200 cisterns have been destroyed or isolated from their owners by construction of the separation barrier, affecting the domestic and agricultural needs of more than 122,000 people.

> "Although [Israelis and Palestinians] share the mountain aquifer that runs the length of the occupied West Bank. Palestinians have access to only a fifth of the water supply, while Israel, which controls the area, takes the rest.
>
> —Rory McCarthy, *The Guardian*, May 27, 2009

> "[N]ever before in history has a large community like this been savaged by bombs and missiles and then denied the means to repair itself." —President Jimmy Carter in Gaza, June 17, 2009, *Arab News*

THE FIRST STRIKE in Israel's Operation "Cast Lead" occurred on December 27, 2008, when 60 Israeli F-16 fighter jets bombed 50 sites in Gaza, killing over 200 Palestinians and wounding close to 1,000 more. During the next 22 days Israel unleashed its full arsenal including phosphorous bombs and cluster bombs on a trapped and largely defenseless civilian population. The ferocity of the attack on civilians and militants alike and the magnitude of the devastation shocked the world.

During the offensive that flattened homes, government buildings, schools, clinics, and refugee camps, the Israeli Defense Ministry closed Israel's border crossings with Gaza and prevented the delivery of United Nations aid shipments. The UN condemned the closure and warned Israel against imposing illegal "collective punishment" against Gaza's 1.5 million residents, most of whom depend on foreign aid. "The Israeli reaction is not justified by those rocket attacks, even though it's caused by those rocket attacks," said John Holmes, undersecretary-general for Humanitarian Affairs.

> "Today's horrific attacks mark only a change in Israel's method of killing Palestinians....In recent months they died mostly silent deaths, the elderly and sick especially, deprived of food and necessary medicine by the two-year-old Israeli blockade calculated and intended to cause suffering and deprivation to 1.5 million Palestinians, the vast majority refugees and children....In Gaza, Palestinians died silently, for want of basic medications...prohibited from reaching them by Israel.

—Ali Abunimah, Electronic Intifada, December 27, 2008

Markets were bombed, farms destroyed. Medical personnel including ambulance drivers were targeted and prevented from evacuating the wounded. Civilian and military areas were targeted, seemingly indiscriminately. As the Israeli assault drew to a close on January 17, demolition squads destroyed all the factories in the northern part of Gaza City.

Israeli officials announced two objectives of the war: to stop Hamas from firing Qassam rockets into Israel, and to eradicate Hamas altogether by killing its militia. Some analysts doubted these stated objectives; a truce between Israel and Hamas had already put an end to Hamas rocket fire. It was recorded that Israel broke the truce on November 4, 2008, by killing six Hamas militia, thus inciting Hamas to resume its rocket fire. Hamas' Qassam rockets are inac-

War on Gaza

Approximately 80% of Gaza's Palestinians are the descendants of the 1948 Nakba from what is now southern Israel—the area of Israel that has come under fire from Gaza militants' home-made Qassam rockets. In the decades since the wars that caused their initial exodus from Israel, many Palestinians have become homeless again during Israeli incursions and home demolitions in Gaza.

Sameh A. Habeeb

e Gaza war in statistics

- ,400 Palestinians killed, including at ast 850 civilians, 350 children, and 110 omen; over 5,000 wounded
- 4 Israelis killed, including 4 civilians, 330 ounded
- ver 4,000 homes destroyed, over 40,000 amaged
- 15 factories and 700 private businesses eriously damaged or destroyed
- 5 hospitals and 43 primary health care enters destroyed or damaged
- 3 government buildings and 60 police ations destroyed or damaged
-) mosques destroyed, 28 damaged
-) schools destroyed and 168 damaged; ree universities/colleges destroyed and 4 damaged
- 3 United Nations properties damaged

curate and contain explosive charges that are small compared to what is contained in a single Israeli shell. In the past eight years, Hamas has launched 8,500 rockets, killing 20 Israelis. By contrast, statistics compiled by the Israeli organization B'Tselem show that between 2000 and December 26, 2008, that is prior to the recent war on Gaza, 3,000 Palestinians in Gaza were killed by Israel forces.

For six months during its truce with Hamas, Israel was planning a war on two fronts—the battlefield and the world press. An opportune moment to launch came during the 2008–2009 Christmas/New Year holiday, which coincided with the Bush–Obama presidential transition.

Commentators around the world asked what military advantage was served by killing and maiming civilians and extensive property destruction. Why would the fourth-most-powerful military in the world seek to destroy the institutions of an imprisoned group of refugees? Perhaps the best clue to Israel's gradual strangulation of the Palestinian people over the past 42 years comes from a remark attributed to Moshe Yaalon, Israeli Defense Forces Chief of Staff in 2002. "The Palestinians must be made to understand in the deepest recesses of their consciousness that they are a defeated people."

On January 22, 2009, Richard Falk, the UN Special Rapporteur—and himself a Jew—declared that Israel's actions against the besieged Gazans were reminiscent of "the worst kind of international memories of the Warsaw Ghetto," a reference to the starvation and murder of Polish Jews by the Nazis. The world is reminded of Israeli historian Ilan Pappe's description of Israeli actions as "a creeping transfer in the West Bank, and a measured genocidal policy in the Gaza strip...."

The Fatah–Hamas power struggle and the Gaza blockade

Beginning in the late 1980s, Israel and the US worked covertly to establish and support Hamas in order to weaken Yasser Arafat. When Hamas candidates won a majority of the seats in the Palestinian parliament in the January 2006 elections, Israel quickly arrested 42 of them—and still holds them in prison. Israel also sealed Gaza in a maneuver to isolate and topple Hamas. Dov Weisglas, advisor to the Israeli Prime Minister, explained that "the idea is to put the Palestinians on a diet, but not make them die of hunger."

In spite of Hamas' election victory in a free and fair election, the US and the EU joined in the boycott of Hamas, demanding that Hamas renounce all violence and recognize Israel's right to exist, but making no reciprocal demands on Israel.

In June 2007, after it became clear that Israel and the US were arming and training elements in Fatah for a military putsch against the elected government, Hamas staged a pre-emptive coup and ousted Fatah militants from Gaza—more than 350 militants died in the skirmishes. Since then several attempts at political unity between the parties have failed. In the meantime, Israel has tightened its blockade of Gaza, depriving the Strip of food, medicines, electricity, fuel, building supplies, and most other necessities.

Palestinians pray on their land prior to the weekly demonstration against the apartheid wall in the West Bank village of Ni'lin, April 10, 2009. Residents of Ni'lin have already lost hundreds of acres to Israeli settlements. The wall would confiscate another 25% of their land.

ALMOST TWO-THIRDS of the estimated nine million Palestinians in the world are refugees or displaced people, the result of massive violence against the Palestinian people. The ethnic cleansing of Palestinian villages and towns at Israel's founding, the demolition of thousands of homes in the decades since, and the tragic statistics on civilian deaths and injuries over years of occupation are ample evidence of the brutality of Israeli policies.

Resistance to oppression is often viewed in the absence of its context, then portrayed as inexplicable barbarity. Some forms of resistance to oppression and colonization are approved in the United Nations charter and in international law and must be distinguished from real terrorism. In the context of the Palestinian struggle for self-determination, this distinction between legitimate resistance and terrorism has been intentionally obfuscated for political ends. In most cases, the media call Palestinian armed resistance "terrorism" while all attacks on Palestinians by the Israeli army are named "self-defense." Little notice is taken of the fact that terror can be "from above" (by the state) and "from below" (by those who resist the violence of the state).

The right of armed resistance to tyranny is a part of the Reformed Tradition and is enshrined in the US Declaration of Independence, as well as various UN resolutions and customary international laws which affirm the legitimacy of armed resistance.

UNGA A/RES/33/24 of November 29, 1978, "Reaffirms the legitimacy of the struggle of peoples for independence, territorial integrity, national unity, and liberation from colonial and foreign domination and foreign occupation by all available means, particularly armed struggle." The principle of self-determination itself provides that, in certain circumstances, force may be used in response to force in the pursuit of self-determination.

Some Palestinian resistance has, indeed, taken forms defined as illegal and illegitimate under international law. In the context of 61 years of ethnic cleansing and violence targeting the Palestinian people collectively, the number of Palestinians engaging in violent resistance is smaller than might be expected. It must be said, however, that such actions have caused grievous harm to individual Israelis and rightly

Resistance to Occupation

Yotam Ronen | Activestills

The agricultural village of Bil'in lies 16 km west of Ramallah. Land belonging to the village has been confiscated in successive stages starting in the 1980s as Jewish settlements were established in the vicinity: Matityahu, Kiryat Sefer, Modi'in Illit, and Matityahu East. In April 2004 Israel began construction of the annexation barrier on the western side of the village, expropriating for its route about 2,300 hectares (575 acres) of Bil'in land.

In response, the people of Bil'in, under the leadership of resident Iyad Burnat, mobilized a campaign of nonviolent resistance involving weekly Friday demonstrations. International and Israeli activists have since joined the campaign in significant numbers. The protests have been occurring regularly for four and a half years; the 225th action occurred in June 2009. Ni'lin, Jayyous, and other villages threatened by land expropria-

Left top: Palestinian demonstrators and their Israeli and international allies face Israeli soldiers at a weekly demonstration in Bil'in in August 2005. Four years later, the demonstrations continue.

Left bottom: Demonstrators run from a teargas cloud shot by the Israeli army during a protest against the apartheid wall in Bil'in on February 20, 2009—the fourth anniversary of the start of protests.

Yotam Ronen | Activestills

tion have taken similar initiatives.

The people of Bil'in have pursued legal options as well. Represented by Michael Sfard, an Israeli human rights lawyer, the village entered a petition to the Israel high court in 2005. The court ruling required the Israeli government to reroute the barrier to expropriate less of the village's land. Such qualified legal "victories" are the excep-

Oren Ziv | Activestills

Some 100 Palestinian demonstrators in Jayyous, joined by Israeli and international activists, march towards the apartheid wall that separates the village from most of its land, November 16, 2008. Farmers are allowed to reach their land only after getting permission from the Israeli army.

drawn near-universal condemnation, including condemnation by Palestinian Christian theologians. (E.g. see Naim Ateek, *Suicide Bombers: What is theologically and morally wrong with suicide bombing?*" Sabeel, 2003.)

Palestinian attempts to gain redress through access to the international bodies that exist for the nonviolent resolution of disputes, including the International Court of Justice and the United Nations, have been stymied, often by US and Israeli combined intransigence. Palestinians have been deprived of legal remedy despite the weight of evidence compiled by international human rights monitoring organizations.

The prepondenance of resistance against Israel's domination has been and is being undertaken by nonviolent means. And yet, the legacy of Palestinian nonviolent resistance is little known—while sensational acts of terrorism have received relentless

attention and define the struggle in the minds of many people unfamiliar with the actuality. Civilian resistance including petitions, strikes, civil disobedience, noncooperation, and boycotts first emerged in the 1920s against the British occupation of Mandate Palestine and its encouragement of Zionist colonial settlement. As early as 1936, Palestinian Christian and Muslim religious leaders were imprisoned for dissenting from Palestine's transformation into a Jewish state. Land Day, begun in 1976 in response to confiscation by the Israeli government of Palestinian land in Galilee, is now observed annually by Palestinian exiles

around the world. The tax revolt of the first intifada began in 1989 in Beit Sahour. The Israeli government has taken many actions to undercut such programs of non-violence, jailing their leaders and forcing others to leave. While many have decried the absence of a "Palestinian Gandhi," the fact is that many are struggling valiantly against heavy odds to be precisely that.

Today, Palestinians whose West Bank villages lie along the path of the separation barrier are engaged in innovative forms of nonviolent resistance in villages, often with the support of Israeli and international allies. Resistance includes "sumud," an Arabic word meaning "steadfastness." Although Israel has intentionally made it difficult to remain on their ancestral lands, Palestinians resist flight and despair by merely surviving day by day with dignity and maintaining a strong social fabric under conditions of profound, chronic stress.

People around the world are acting in support of Palestinian nonviolent resistance to occupation. Since the governments of many western nations support Israeli oppression with financial assistance and diplomatic influence, a global movement for boycotts, divestment, and sanctions has been initiated.

tion to the rule and, at that, have minimal impact on the ongoing Israeli land-grab.

In July 2008 Bil'in commenced legal proceedings in Canadian courts against Green Park International Inc. and Green Mount International Inc., two Canadian corporations involved in the construction, marketing, and sale of settlement housing units in Modi'in Illit.

Above: Israeli soldiers arrest a Palestinian man who tried to block them from shooting tear gas canisters toward the crowd of demonstrators during a protest against the apartheid wall in Bil'in on April 24, 2009. Hundreds of Palestinians, Israelis, and internationals protested the murder of Bassam Ibrahim Abu Rahma, who was killed by an Israeli solider during the Friday demonstration a week earlier.

Left: Friends of Bassam Ibrahim Abu Rahma gather at his grave after his funeral in Bil'in on April 18, 2009. Abu Rahma, 30, was killed in a confrontation with border policemen during a protest on April 17 after being shot with an extended-range teargas projectile aimed directly at his chest at close range. He was critically injured and died shortly after arriving at a hospital in Ramallah.

> "The context that is often missing from the current reporting is that the Palestinian uprising is a revolt against a 34-year-long occupation. If there is no occupation in the story, then the story doesn't really make sense.

—Alisa Solomon, *Peace, Propaganda and the Promised Land*, 2001

Part Three: Responses

THE ECONOMICS OF THE OCCUPATION

33   The US role in sustaining occupation

34   Socially responsible economic engagement

CHRISTIAN ENGAGEMENT FOR CHANGE

36   Mission in partnership

37   Church-based initiatives for change

RESOURCES

40   Timeline of the conflict

42   Resources for further study

43   A leaders' guide to using this resource

Over the past three or four decades, in spite of Israel's illegal occupation and confiscation of Palestinian land, the United States has provided unwavering diplomatic and financial support for Israel. The Obama administration has signalled an intention to change course, but meaningful change that alters the facts on the ground is not likely to happen without grassroots engagement by Americans whose taxes support the Israeli occupation and whose votes elect the politicians who determine our foreign policy.

The Presbyterian Church (U.S.A.) has a longstanding commitment to peacemaking activities in Palestine/Israel on multiple fronts, including ameliorating the conditions of Palestinians' lives and advocating for a just peace. These activities and relationships have been sustained by General Assembly resolutions dating from 1948 forward, by program funds to support personnel and programs in the Holy Land, and by participation in the ecumenical bodies of the Middle East.

Martha

As awareness grows, more individuals and organizations committed to the pursuit of just peace for Palestinians and Isra find constructive ways of engagement. In the United States, Presbyterians are working within the church and building bri with others in actions like this vigil in protest of Israel's siege and assault of Gaza. The vigil, which took place on Januar 2009 in Oak Park, Illinois, brought together Christians, Jews, Muslims, and others and drew some 75 participants.

> "Since 1948, the Presbyterian Church General Assembly has called repeatedly for a just peace that respects the rights and needs of both Israelis and Palestinians. The Amman Call of 2007 demands of us a fresh commitment. Palestinian Christians—from Gaza to Jerusalem to Nazareth—are urging us as their brothers and sisters in Christ to act with speed and determination. "Enough is enough," they say. "No more words without deeds. It is time for action."

The economics of the occupation

The US role in sustaining the Israeli occupation

On MAY 18, 2009, President Obama and Israeli Prime Minister Benjamin Netanyahu met at the White House to discuss the conditions necessary for peace in the Middle East. The result was a clash of world views between the two governments—the first major clash in many years.

The US relationship with Israel has been one whereby the US has turned a blind eye to Israel's breach of international law and negotiated agreements with the Palestinians.

Political pressure from military contractors, oil companies, construction and high-tech companies, neo-conservative ideologues, Christian Zionists, and the "Israel Lobby" have combined to provide almost uncondi-

President George W. Bush (shown here with Knesset speaker Dalia Itzik) traveled in May 2008 to Israel to mark its 60th anniversary. Bush addressed a special session of the Israeli parliament, affirming that the United States was "proud to be Israel's closest ally and best friend." Historically, the US-Israel "special relationship" has taken the form of uncritical diplomatic support and unrestricted funding.

fad I EPA

tional support in Congress for whatever the Israeli government says and does. No US president to date has been able to to consistently or effectively resist that pressure for long.

The US diplomatic monopoly of the conflict serves to advance Israel's goals. Diplomatic protection buffers Israel from international scrutiny and

perpetuates the "peace process gridlock" that allows the Israeli government to negotiate indefinitely while intensifying the occupation.

Military aid to Israel

In the mid-1960s, US aid to Israel averaged $63 million per year; by 1971 the annual allocation was increased ten-fold to $634.5 million; after the Yom Kippur War in 1973, Congress bumped up US aid to over $3 billion per year. In recent years the level has remained at $3 billion in direct assistance. This amounts to one-sixth of all US foreign aid and 2% of the Israeli budget. On average, the US gave more than $6.8 million to Israel *each day* during 2007.

At present, aid takes the form of military aid. At the end of the fiscal year, the US Congress often converts that year's loans to Israel into grants. Every other country is required to account for how US aid is spent—not Israel.

US aid has been used to support Israel's military occupation of Palestine, to build illegal colonies and segregated highways on Palestinian lands, to construct what Palestinians call the apartheid wall, to pulverize Lebanon in 1982 and again in 2006, and devastate West Bank cities in 2002. The primary weapons used in the Israeli assault on Gaza in December-January 2008-2009 were American-made: F-16s, Blackhawk and Apache helicopters, and Caterpillar D-9 bulldozers.

In August 2007 the Bush Administration announced a new ten-year agreement that it would increase US military assistance to Israel by $6 billion over the next decade.

> "Without concrete consequences for Tel Aviv's noncompliance—such as withholding all or part of the $3 billion annual US military aid to Israel, or withdrawing the US diplomatic protection that keeps Israel from being held accountable in the UN Security Council—Obama's demands for a settlement freeze or anything else will have little impact.

—Phyllis Bennis, Z Space, June 17, 2009

Palestinians see a blatant double standard in US diplomatic and financial support for Israel's occupation. The security pretext for Israel's annexation/apartheid barrier obscures the daily fact of the occupation. In depriving its victims of their human rights, freedom, and dignity, the occupation is itself an extreme form of violence and oppression, to which Palestinian violence is an understandable response.

> "During negotiations, [the United States] rarely if ever adopt[s] objectively neutral or equidistant positions between Israel and the Arabs. Indeed, we often operate on peace process software that automatically adjusts our position in light of Israel's needs and concerns....This pro-Israel posture makes us a partial mediator.

—Aaron David Miller, Middle East analyst, author, and negotiator, *The Long Dance: Searching for Arab-Israeli Peace*, Woodrow Wilson International Center for Scholars

Diplomatic support for the occupation

Since 1972 the US has vetoed over 42 UN Security Council resolutions criticizing Israel for breaches of international law. The US Congress frequently passes resolutions in support of Israeli military actions like attacks in Lebanon in 2002 and 2006 and the attack on Gaza in 2008—offensives that mock the moral principle of proportionality and outrage much of the rest of the world.

Furthermore, the US has turned a blind eye to Israel's 200 or so nuclear weapons and put no pressure on Israel to permit site inspections of its nuclear facilities. Nor has the US condemned Israel's active chemical and biological weapons program. It is as though different rules apply to Israel alone.

In light of what has transpired over

Secretary of State Condoleezza Rice registered objections in June 2008 to Israel's plans to build 1,300 homes in East Jerusalem Jewish settlements, calling them "simply not helpful" to peace efforts in the region. "We've talked a great deal about road map obligations, and this one isn't being met," Rice said. Despite Israel's disregard for US concerns, aid is not conditional on compliance and continues to flow to Israel unhindered.

CONDOLEEZZA RICE
SECRETARY OF STATE

"The irony is hard to miss....[T]he United States has pressured many other states to join the NPT [Non-Proliferation Treaty], imposed sanctions on countries that have defied US wishes and acquired nuclear weapons anyway, gone to war in 2003 to prevent Iraq from pursuing WMD, and contemplated attacking Iran and North Korea for the same reason. Yet Washington has long subsidized an ally whose clandestine WMD activities are well-known and whose nuclear arsenal has given several of its neighbors a powerful incentive to seek WMD themselves.

The most singular feature of US support for Israel is its increasingly unconditional nature....Since the mid-1960s, Israel has continued receiving generous support even when it took actions American leaders thought were unwise and contrary to US interests....It gets its aid when it builds settlements in the occupied territories... even though the US government opposes this policy. It also gets its aid when it annexes territory it has conquered,...sells US military technology to potential enemies like China, conducts espionage operations on US soil, or uses US weapons in ways that violate US Law....And it gets its aid even when Israeli leaders renege on pledges made to US presidents.

Excerpted from *The Israel Lobby* by John Mearsheimer and Stephen Walt

Socially responsible economic engagement

THE PRESBYTERIAN CHURCH (U.S.A.) has been a leader in the field of socially responsible investment since the early 1970s with the creation of a special committee on Mission Responsibility Through Investment (MRTI). The church is now engaged in studying where and how its money is used, and takes action to promote better corporate practices. Currently, environmental concerns and human rights violations are the most urgent reasons for negotiations with corporations, stockholder resolutions, and divestment from offending companies.

Since 1967, many Israeli and international corporations have made huge profits from the military occupation of Palestine. Corporations profit from the Israeli occupation whenever they do business in illegal settlements. For example, Blockbuster and Ace Hardware have stores in Ma'ale Adumim, a settlement that was established on a hilltop east of the Green Line in 1975 by 23 Israeli families and now has a population of 35,000.

Corporations also profit from the construction of illegal settlements, the infrastructure that supports them, and the barriers that claim Palestinian land for the use of Jewish settlements.

Two American companies that the PC(USA) Committee on MRTI is engaging to end their role in the occupation are Caterpillar and Motorola.

CAT equipment has demolished thousands of homes, uprooted countless olive trees, and carved gaping holes in roads to make them impassable. In addition, CAT equipment and

Above: To date, Caterpillar Corporation has resisted demands from institutional money managers, shareholders, and human rights activists to cease business practices that contribute to and profit from the occupation.

similar machines from other manufacturers are used in the construction of settlement housing, segregated roads on expropriated land, and the annexation/apartheid barrier—all violations of international law.

Motorola Corporation also contributes to the occupier's control of the Palestinian population. Motorola's radar detection devices and thermal cameras protect illegal Israeli settlements; its "Mountain Rose" secure cell phone communication system enhances the coordination and monitoring capabilities of Israel's occupying forces; and Motorola's Wide Area Surveillance System (WASS), which was recently sold to an Israeli company, is used to monitor and maintain the apartheid barrier.

A comprehensive strategy

Corporations that profit from Israel's occupation are under pressure

the past 42 years, it is hard to dispute the charge that the US has not been an honest broker between Israelis and Palestinians. Many have concluded that change in the "facts on the ground" in Israel/Palestine will occur only when the "facts on the ground" in the US are changed.

Right: While Israel defends its right to "natural growth" in expanding settlements built on occupied territory, tens of thousands of Palestinian houses in East Jerusalem and the West Bank face demolition because they were built without a permit. This bureaucratic formula for circumscribing "natural growth" in Palestinian communities gives Israel's practice of bulldozing Palestinian homes a veneer of legitimacy because only "illegal" houses are demolished. Building permits are nearly impossible for Palestinians to obtain. The armored D-9 Caterpillar seen here is used in military actions and provided to Israel as a part of the Pentagon's Foreign Military Financing program.

to change. In 2005 more than 170 Palestinian coalitions, unions, refugee groups, and human rights and social justice groups issued a call to the world to engage in comprehensive BDS (boycott by consumers, divestment by investors, and sanctions by governments) against Israel until Israel ends the occupation and complies with international law.

Churches and other institutions are taking steps to examine the connection between their investments and corporate involvement in the Israeli occupation. In 2005 the Church of Ireland divested from Cement Roadstone Holdings because of the company's involvement in the Wall construction. In 2008 the American Friends Service Committee adopted screens for their investments directly linked to the occupation and violence.

In December 2008 the Church of England divested from Caterpillar. In February 2009 Hampshire College became the first US college or university to divest from Caterpillar, United Technologies, General Electric, ITT Corporation, Motorola, and Terex. Under pressure from pro-Israel groups both institutions claimed their decisions were made for financial, not moral reasons.

In May 2009 20 different Israeli organizations issued an appeal for the withdrawal of the Norwegian national pension fund's investments in all Israeli and international corporations which are involved in the Israeli occupation of Palestinian territories.

In the US, church groups, municipal governments, university groups, and advocacy organizations are employing BDS-related strategies.

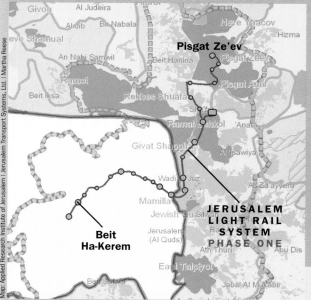

Map: Applied Research Institute of Jerusalem | Jerusalem Transport Systems, Ltd. | Martha Reese

JERUSALEM LIGHT RAIL SYSTEM PHASE ONE

Pisgat Ze'ev

Beit Ha-Kerem

Left: Phase one of Jerusalem's massive rail transit project will link the Jewish settlement of Pisgat Ze'ev in the West Bank with Beit Ha-Kerem in Israel. Israel redrew the municipal boundaries of Jerusalem in 1967 in the first phase of its project to annex and Judaize "Greater Jerusalem." The strategic placement of Jewish settlements severs Jerusalem from its Palestinian hinterland. The rail system, built across expropriated land to serve settlements constructed on expropriated land, is designed to consolidate Israeli control over the region. In the map at left, the yellow-shaded areas lie outside Israel's border, the Green Line.

Right: In the master plan for Jerusalem's regional light rail network, the portions of the system outside the white area are beyond Israel's internationally-recognized border along the Green Line.

A victory for BDS: Veolia withdraws from controversial Jerusalem light rail system

In 2003 the French corporation Veolia Transportation/Connex was awarded a $500 million contract to build and operate a light railway to serve Jerusalem and vicinity. The first line slated for construction is planned to link the Jewish settlement of Pisgat Ze'ev to Beit Ha-Kerem in Israel. The entire rail system, when completed, will include eight lines and is scheduled to be fully functional in 2020.

As news spread of Veolia's participation in the controversial project, public pressure mounted for Veolia to pull out of the project. According to various reports, the firm lost major projects in Europe—such as the contract to operate the Stockholm Metro—because of popular outrage over its involvement in the Jerusalem project.

Veolia also faced legal challenges. A lawsuit in the French courts brought by a Palestinian advocacy organization demanded that Veolia abandon the light rail project based on an article in French law that allows the court to void business

Atarot Airport

Neve Ya'akov

Pisgat Ze'ev

Ramot

Har Ha-Ttzofim Campus

Old City

JERUSALEM LIGHT RAIL SYSTEM DEVELOPMENT PLAN

Gilo

Jerusalem Maas Transit System Project | Martha Reese

agreements signed by French companies that violate international law.

In June 2009 Veolia abandoned the project and is trying to find a buyer for its stake in the project. Activists have hailed Veolia's decision and are celebrating a major victory in the Boycott, Sanctions, and Divestment movement targeting corporations that profit from Israel's settlement and occupation enterprise.

Mission in partnership

Presbyterians do mission in partnership!" This fundamental tenet of our denomination is particularly relevant in Palestine, where our partners live under great stress. Partnership provides them with the ongoing encouragement that comes from knowing that fellow Christians around the world understand their situation and pray regularly for them.

We seek to "walk with" our partners: to learn from them, encourage them, and be guided in our actions by them. Staying in relationship can also equip the American partners with regular, up-to-date information as events unfold.

Our denomination has long-standing partnerships with various ecumenical bodies in Palestine: Episcopal, Lutheran, Orthodox, and Catholic; the Middle East Council of Churches (MECC); and other church and para-church organizations.

Many delegations explore our denomination's deep roots and long-term links with religious, educational, and health projects by meeting and worshiping with fellow Christians while they are there.

In Gaza, Presbyterian Disaster Assistance (PDA) works with Action by Churches Together (ACT), a global alliance of 175 churches and related organizations working worldwide to support communities in emergencies. The Department of Service to Palestinian Refugees of the MECC provides up-to-date information on the situation of Palestinian refugees in the

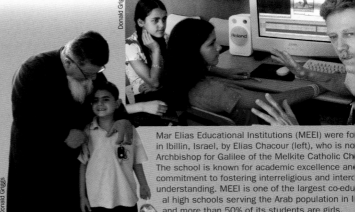

Mar Elias Educational Institutions (MEEI) were fo[unded] in Ibillin, Israel, by Elias Chacour (left), who is no[w] Archbishop for Galilee of the Melkite Catholic Ch[urch]. The school is known for academic excellence an[d] commitment to fostering interreligious and interc[ultural] understanding. MEEI is one of the largest co-edu[cation]al high schools serving the Arab population in I[srael], and more than 50% of its students are girls.

Partnerships in Israel/Palestine

- For further information about partnerships, see www.israelpalestinemissionnetwork.org/partnerships.

- A full list of our denomination's partners in Israel/Palestine can be found at www.pcusa.org/worldwide/israelpalestine/international.htm.

- To make a financial contribution through the denomination's Extra Commitment Opportunities (ECOs) in Israel and Palestine, go to www.pcusa.org/worldwide/israelpalestine/giving.htm.

- For gifts in response to emergency and crisis situations, go to www.pcusa.org/pda.

- For denominational guidelines for partnerships, see www.pcusa.org/worldwide/get-involved/protocols.htm.

- For advice on partnering in Israel/Palestine, contact Victor Makari (Victor.Makari@pcusa.org) or Donald Mead at the Israel/Palestine Mission Network (mead@msu.edu).

Below: The International Center of Bethlehem started in 1994 as an outreach ministry of Christmas Lutheran Church with a budget of $327. The exponential and inspirational growth of the organization is partly a result of committed partnerships with American Christians. Rev. Dr. Mitri Raheb, its general director, has overseen the growth of the Center's celebrated arts and crafts program.

Memorial PC, Midland, MI, has given strong support to the music program at Dar al-Kalima College at the International Center in Bethlehem, including support for a new practice building and a new music computer lab. They are providing scholarships for two students at the College's school of fine arts. Several people from the College have visited their church in Michigan; they hope to arrange a mission trip to Bethlehem soon. Contact Marilyn Wildes at marilyn-wildes@sbcglobal.net.

North Creek PC, Mill Creek, WA, is working with Bethlehem Bible College to help develop an Information Technology infrastructure to confront the pervasive economic hardships, enabling students to work in areas that provide IT employment. Contact: Joe Upton at peg.joe@verizon.net.

Lafayette-Orinda PC, Lafayette, CA, has visited and given strong support over the years to two organizations in Gaza: Ahli Arab Hospital and the Atfaluna Society for Deaf Children. They also participate in partnership with the Pilgrims of Ibillin in supporting the Mar Elias Educational Institutions and are faithful supporters of our Regional Liaison, Douglas Dicks. Contact: Tom Francis at thfrancis@deloitte.com.

Presbytery of Greater Atlanta. This presbytery's partnership, through the Presbyterian Hunger Program, is with a consortium of six church and para-church organizations in Palestine: the International Center in Bethlehem, Bethlehem Bible College, Wi'am, the YWCA, Democracy and Workers Rights Center in Ramallah, and the Palestine Working Women's Society for Development. For more information, contact Sarah Humphrey at answertohunger@bellsouth.com.

Since 1999, **Philadelphia Presbytery** has had a partnership with the Diocese of Jerusalem of the Episcopal Church of Jerusalem and the Middle East. The Presbytery has initiated many reciprocal visits with church partners in Palestine and Israel as well as in Jordan and Lebanon. Their members have been active participants in a nine-denomination Ecumenical Working Group for Middle East Peace, hosting conferences and workshops. Contact Rev. David Yeaworth (d.yeaworth@world-net.att.net).

Keep Hope Alive is a Peacemaking

Church-based iniatives for change

whole of Israel, the occupied territories, and Gaza.

Many Presbyterians travel to Israel and Palestine seeking to deepen their spiritual roots. Direct, personal experience builds awareness of the conflict that engulfs both Israelis and Palestinians. Upon returning home, they are anxious to learn more, share what they have learned, and influence the policies of our church and our nation. Many experience an irresistible urge to return to Israel/Palestine —and do.

ogram of three
n Francisco Bay
ea Presbyteries, in
rtnership with the
CA of East Jeru-
lem and the YWCA
Palestine. Each
ar, two delegations
to the West Bank
help Palestinian
milies plant olive
es (February) and
rvest olives (Oc-
er). Contact Walt
vis, waltandlibby@
mcast.net.

any congregations
ve ongoing links
th the **Sabeel Ecu-**

menical Liberation Theology Center in Jerusalem, facilitated through **Friends of Sabeel North America** (www.fosna.org). This group sponsors regular conferences in the US and in Palestine.

Other churches have links with **Mar Elias Educational Institutions**, established through the initiative of Archbishop Elias Chacour in Ibillin, Israel. These links are facilitated by the US organization, **Pilgrims of Ibillin** (www.pilgrimsofibillin.org).

Thanks in part to a strong partnership with Memorial PC in Midland, MI, the music program at Dar al-Kalima College at the International Center in Bethlehem has well-equipped practice facilities for its students.

PC(USA) General Assembly statements from 1948 to 2003

Since 1948 Presbyterian General Assemblies have repeatedly addressed issues of relevance to the Middle East, particularly Israel and Palestine. Consistent with UN resolutions, the Church has affirmed the right of Israel to exist as a sovereign state within secure, internationally-recognized borders; affirmed the right of Palestinians to self-determination, including the right to the establishment of a viable, independent, sovereign state; and condemned acts of terrorism and other acts of violence against innocent people by all parties to the conflict.

The Assembly has also demanded an end to the occupation; a return to the pre-1967 borders (the "Green Line" set by the UN in 1949); the removal of all Israeli settlements on Palestinian land, or a one-for-one exchange of land; the removal of the Separation Barrier to the Israeli side of the border; the right of return of Palestinian refugees and their descendants and compensation for their losses; and an international Jerusalem shared by both Israel and Palestine.

PC(USA) General Assembly statements from 2004-2008

The 216th, 217th, and 218th General Assemblies have struggled mightily with issues related to peace and justice in Israel and Palestine. This struggle can be best summarized by saying that the Presbyterian Church (U.S.A.) unequivocally stands for peace and justice in Israel/Palestine, but is divided about how to best approach specific issues related to that goal. Our historical relationships with Palestinians, Israelis, and the American Jewish community have complicated our attempts to speak with one prophetic voice. The following is a brief description of General Assembly actions in

the past four years that are relevant to this denominational conversation. (All references to General Assembly actions can be found on official Presbyterian website pages.)

The 216th General Assembly (2004) directed the "formation of a Worldwide Ministries Division-related Palestine Mission Network...for the purpose of creating currents of wider and deeper Presbyterian involvement with Palestinian partners, aimed at demonstrating solidarity and changing the conditions that erode the humanity of Palestinians."

The same decision which called for the creation of the Palestine Mission Network also called for a "systematic effort of development and compassionate action in Palestine." That decision provided the impetus for the network's activities relating to travel and marketing of products, as well as a search for opportunities for pro-active investment in affordable housing and in other areas that could contribute to economic improvement. Those efforts are ongoing.

The Assembly also called upon the Stated Clerk to issue a pastoral letter on Christian Zionism and the ongoing conflict in Israel and Palestine and to post it on the PC(USA) website; directed the General Assembly Council "to develop a brief resource and study guide to assist Presbyterians in understanding how biblical faith and Reformed theology guide our understanding of present realities and possibilities in the Middle East"; requested the Stated Clerk to "make known" the church's opposition to the construction of a wall and other barriers by the State of Israel and the desire that the United States make no monetary contribution to its $1.3 billion construction cost; called for an end to Israel's occupation of Palestinian Territories; condemned "horrific acts of violence and deadly attacks on innocent people" by both sides; called on the United States government to be an "honest broker" in working toward peace in the region; and referred to the Mission Responsibility Through Investment Committee "instructions to initiate a process of phased, selective divestment in multinational corporations operating in Israel, in accordance to General Assembly policy on social investing...."

The 217th General Assembly (2006) acknowledged the hurt and misunderstanding in the Jewish community regarding actions of the 216th General Assembly and asked for "a new season of mutual understanding and dialogue," replaced the 2004 wording regarding divestment with instructions to the Mission Responsibility Through Investment (MRTI) Committee to assure that the finan-

cial resources of the PC(USA) "be invested in only peaceful pursuits," and affirmed MRTI as the appropriate vehicle for achieving this goal.

The Assembly also called upon the church to work for an end to all violence and terror against Palestinian and Israeli civilians; to work for an end to the the occupation; and to work toward the creation of a secure Palestinian State alongside a secure Israeli State, stating that it did not believe the PC(USA) "should tell a sovereign nation whether it can protect its borders or handle matters of national defense."

In addition to the statements mentioned on page 3 of this resource, The 218th General Assembly (2008)

directed GA offices to develop appropriate resources regarding Just Peace in Israel and Palestine; called for continued "corporate engagement with companies supporting or profiting from the occupation of Palestine and/or other violence in the region"; called upon the church to "be a voice for the victims of violence in both Israel and Palestine...[and not] over-identify with the realities of the Israelis and Palestine [but with] the need for peacemaking voices in the midst of horrific acts of violence and terror"; and rejected attempts to limit the work of General Assembly staff, organizations, and entities in regard to advocating for a Just Peace in Israel and Palestine.

The Amman Call, an ecumenical statement

" The Palestinian Christians, from Gaza to Jerusalem and to Nazareth, have called out to their brothers and sisters in Christ with this urgent plea: 'Enough is enough. No more words without deeds. It is time for action.'

So begins the World Council of Churches' "Amman Call" of June 2007 when more than 130 representatives from six continents agreed on a new effort to re-energize the worldwide church's response to the 60 years of turmoil following the establishment of the state of Israel. The 218th (2008) General Assembly of the Presbyterian Church (U.S.A.) endorsed the Amman Call and instructed that it be considered in any study processes of the church (http://www.pc-biz.org/Explorer.aspx?id=1429). Below are excerpts from this call of our brothers and sisters in Christ in the Holy Land.

"Almost sixty years have passed since the Christian churches first spoke with one voice about Arab-Israeli peace. For the last forty years the Christian churches have called for an end to the Israeli occupation of Palestine. In the very place where Jesus Christ walked upon the earth,

walls now separate families and the children of God—Christian, Muslim and Jew—are imprisoned in a deepening cycle of violence, humiliation and despair.

"We welcome the timely and prophetic statement of the Heads of Churches in Jerusalem. We affirm that 'the Churches are part of the conflict, because the Churches cannot remain silent while there is still suffering. The role of the Churches is to heal and to bring all sides to reconciliation.' Our belief in God reminds us 'that all God's children of all religions and political parties are to be respected.' We assure the Churches of Palestine and Israel of our prayers, collaboration and resources.

"[We affirm:] that UN resolutions are the basis for peace and the Geneva conventions are applicable to the rights and responsibilities of the affected people; that Palestinians have the right of self-determination

and the right of return; that a two-state solution must be viable politically, geographically economically and socially; that Jerusalem must be an open, accessible, inclusive and shared city for the two peoples and three religions; that both Palestine and Israel have legitimate security needs; that the Israeli settlements in the occupied Palestinian territories are illegal, and constitute an obstacle to peace; that the 'Separation Barrier' constructed by Israel in the occupied Palestinian territories is a grave breach of international law and must be removed from the occupied territory; that there is no military solution for this conflict. Violence in all its forms cannot be justified whether perpetrated by Israelis or Palestinians; that comprehensive regional peace is indivisible from a just peace in Israel and Palestine; that the life and witness of local churches is at the center of worldwide church advocacy for a just peace."

The memory of the *Nakba* (Arabic for "Catastrophe") shapes present-day consciousness and identity. As Americans learn about the Jewish and Palestinian "narratives," they also learn of Palestinian resentment about what they perceive as a double standard in the acceptance of their collective narrative. Palestinians observe that Jewish efforts to preserve the memory of their collective experience and *Shoah* (Hebrew for "Catastrophe") are met with respect and acceptance, while Palestinians are urged to "stop living in the past" and "move on."

Tamal Akham's painting (above) shows the expulsion of Palestinians through the port of Jaffa in 1948. Over 85,000 Palestinians living in Haifa and Jaffa at the time were forced to flee through the Mediterranean seaports. Some tried in desperation to escape on small fishing boats; those who found no place in the crowded boats were lost overboard.

Left: An Israeli affiliated with Anarchists Against the Wall walks hand in hand with a Kufr Qadum villager in a peaceful demonstration against encroachment by the nearby settlements Kedumim and Kedumim Ilit.

Anna Baltzer

Left: Combatants for Peace is a group of former combat soldiers in the Israel Defense Forces and former fighters in the Palestinian liberation struggle. Today, these men share the belief that the conflict cannot be resolved through violence and occupation. In April 2009 a group of Israelis with the organization passed through Israeli checkpoints to enter the West Bank for a meeting and conversation with their Palestinian counterparts. (www.combatantsforpeace.org)

Yotam Ronen / Activestills

A tribute to Israeli peacemakers

Israeli activists are working creatively and courageously to foster the conditions for just peace. As ever-greater numbers of Israelis and Palestinians work together in nonviolent resistance to occupation, they are building the foundations for a future that embraces the interdependency of all who share the land. These photographs document the activities of only a few of the countless Israeli individuals and organizations from whose important work we draw inspiration and resolve.

Left: In January 2007 the acclaimed Israeli human rights organization B'Tselem launched its camera distribution project in the occupied territories. The camera enabled 14-year-old Fida' Abu 'Ayesha to capture on film numerous incidents of severe harassment in 2006 and 2007 perpetrated by extremist settlers who live in Tel Rumeida across the street from her house in Hebron. View it and others at www.btselem.org.

Don't you dare film me!

Below: Jeff Halper and Meir Margalit of the Israeli Committee Against House Demolitions attempt to prevent the demolition of a Palestinian home in Silwan, Jerusalem, in January 2008. (www.icahd.org)

ICAHD

...e: Israeli activists from Ta'ayush are sometimes present to intercede ...ses of violence and harrassment against Palestinian villagers by ...ers and soldiers in the rural South Hebron area. In July 2001 the ...ers, fences, and baking ovens of five Palestinian villages in the area ...demolished; then soldiers and civil administration workers poured ...s into the wells that served as the villagers' only source of water. ...e then Ta'ayush activists have led periodic convoys to bring food and ...r to the now-homeless Palestinians. (www.taayush.org)

Left: Israel is focused on uncovering the archaeological record of Jewish history as validation for its contemporary political claim. Since 1948 Israel's policies have deliberately erased and obscured the traces of the land's absent Palestinians. Zochrot ("Remembering" in Hebrew) is raising awareness among Israeli Jews of the history of Palestinians in the land. (www.zochrot.org)

Oren Ziv / Activestills

...w: Consisting of
...ral hundred bereaved
...ies, half of them
...stinian and half Israeli,
...arents Circle–Families
...n was founded in
...s to foster reconcilia-
...between Israelis and
...stinians beginning with
...embers—all of whom
...lost immediate family
...bers to the violence
...e region. (www.thepar-
...circle.org)

Right: MachsomWatch (*machsom* is Hebrew for "checkpoint") was founded in 2001 by Israeli women opposed to the Israeli occupation of the territories and the systematic repression of the Palestinians who live there. MachsomWatch members often take positions at checkpoints to monitor and attempt intervention in cases of abuse. MachsomWatch's videos on YouTube give a compelling insider's view of anti-occupation activism. (www.machsomwatch.org)

Keren Manor / Activestills

Above: In January 1988 a small group of Israeli women began a simple form of protest: once a week at the same time and place they donned black clothing and raised hand-shaped signs containing the message "Stop the Occupation." Now, weekly vigils are held in Gan-Shmuel, Haifa, Jerusalem, Carmiel, Nachshon, and Tel-Aviv.

Martha Reese

A historical overview

Pre 1947—The Zionist beginnings

1897. First Zionist Conference meets in Basel, Switzerland, with goal of establishing a national Jewish homeland in historic Palestine where, at the time, Jews make up less than 2% of the population.

1914. The Ottoman Empire enters World War I on the side of Germany.

1917. Britain signs the Balfour Declaration supporting the "establishment in Palestine of a national home for the Jewish people...it being clearly understood that nothing shall be done which may prejudice the civil and religious rights of existing non-Jewish communities in Palestine...."

> In Palestine we do not propose to go through the form of consulting the wishes of the present inhabitants.... The four great powers are committed to Zionism and Zionism...is rooted in age-long tradition, in present needs, in future hopes, of far profounder import than the desires and prejudices of the 700,000 Arabs who now inhabit that ancient land.

—Lord Balfour, British Foreign Secretary, author of the Balfour Declaration, 1919

1918. World War I ends, bringing the defeat of the Ottoman Empire.

1920s. League of Nations grants Britain a mandate over Palestine and Jordan. Palestinian general labor strike and violent attacks protest Zionist immigration.

1939-47. Jewish immigration escalates in response to Nazi persecution and atrocities in Europe. In protest of British efforts to restrict immigration, Zionists organize underground gangs that attack British and Palestinian officials and civilians. Palestinian opposition to Zionism continues.

1947-1948—War of Independence and Arab cleansing

1947. The UN General Assembly passes Resolution 181, which would partition Palestine into Jewish and Arab states and establish Greater Jerusalem as an international city. The Jewish state would receive 56% of the land of the Palestine Mandate, the Arab state about 44%. Zionist leaders accept the plan; Palestinians reject it. Riots and fighting break out.

1948. Recognizing the impossibility of establishing a Jewish state in a land with a non-Jewish majority, Zionist forces launch a series of operations that induce the flight of some 750,000 Palestinians (75% of the indigenous Palestinian population). British withdraw as mandate ends. On May 14 Zionists declare Israel a Jewish State, and gain recognition by the United Nations. Egypt, Syria, Iraq, Lebanon, Jordan, and Saudi Arabia declare war on Israel. The war results in a divided Jerusalem and 531 "cleansed" Arab villages. Palestinian refugee camps are established in Lebanon, Syria, Jordan, Egypt, and in the areas now known as the West Bank and Gaza. In December the United Nations adopts the "Universal Declaration of Human Rights" and UN Resolution 194, stating that "refugees wishing to return to their homes and live at peace with their neighbors should be permitted to do so at the earliest practicable date, and those wishing not to return should be compensated for their property."

1949-1967—Consolidation

1949. Initial borders are established along what will become known as the Green Line, encompassing nearly 50% more territory into Israel than was originally allotted by the UN Partition Plan, a total of 78% of historic Palestine. West Bank and Gaza come under Jordanian and Egyptian control, respectively.

1953. Israel illegally begins to divert the waters of the Jordan River. In response President Eisenhower suspends all economic aid to Israel.

1964. The Palestine Liberation Organization (PLO) is established, advocating armed struggle for liberation.

1967. In a pre-emptive strike, Israel attacks Egypt, Syria, Iraq, and Jordan and in six days occupies the West Bank, Gaza, Sinai, Golan Heights, and the Arab sector of East Jerusalem. About 320,000 Palestinians are displaced, more than half of them for the second time. Israel immediately establishes Jewish-only settlements in the West Bank, Gaza, and East Jerusalem. In November the UN Security Council passes Resolution 242, stressing the "inadmissibility of the acquisition of territory by war" and calling for the "withdrawal of Israeli armed forces from territories occupied" and a "just settlement to the refugee problem."

1968-1992—Military occupation

1968-69. Fatah gains formal control of the PLO; Yassir Arafat becomes chair.

1973. On the Jewish holy day of Yom Kippur, Egypt and Syria attack Israel. With significant US economic and military assistance, Israel, although losing nearly 150 planes and suffering hundreds of casualties, pushes back both armies.

1974. The Arab League declares the PLO to be the only legitimate representative of the Palestinian people. The UN recognizes the Palestinians' right to sovereignty and grants observer status to the PLO.

1978. Egypt and Israel in the Camp David Accords reach a peace agreement, providing for the return of the Sinai to Egypt in exchange for recognition of Israel. Israel invades Lebanon, occupying its southern border in response to the violence of the PLO.

Martha Reese

1980. Israel declares Jerusalem its eternal, undivided capital, affirming the 1967 annexation of East Jerusalem.

1981. Israel annexes the Golan Heights.

1982. Israel invades Lebanon a second time, laying siege to Beirut. The PLO moves its headquarters to Tunis. Hezbollah (Party of God) comes into existence to counter the Israeli invasion. Beirut is occupied by Israel.

1982. Israeli troops under command of Ariel Sharon encircle the Sabra-Shatilla Palestinian refugee camp in southern Beirut, allowing Lebanese Phalangist (Maronite Christian) troops to enter the camp and massacre thousands of women, children, and elderly men over a period of several days.

1983. Israel and Lebanon sign agreement terminating the state of war and recognizing the border. Arafat and PLO leadership, forced to leave, go to Tunis until 1994.

1985. The Israeli government orders the withdrawal of its troops from most of Lebanon. Israeli troops remain in southern Lebanon until 2000.

1987. The first Intifada, a Palestinian popular uprising, begins in Gaza and spreads to the West Bank. The uprising is crushed by Israelis.

1988. The PLO accepts UN Security Council Resolutions 242 and 338, implicitly recognizing Israel. The United States opens dialogue with the PLO. The Hamas Islamic Brotherhood is

founded with a charter advocating the destruction of Israel.

1992. President George H. W. Bush's administration holds up ten billion dollars in US loan guarantees to Israel in an attempt to limit Israeli settlement building.

1993-2009—The "Peace Process"

1993. Israel and the PLO sign the Oslo Declaration of Principles, which provide for mutual recognition. The PLO renounces violence and the use of terrorism and agrees to revise the PLO Charter to remove chapters referring to the destruction of Israel.

1994. A Jewish American settler in Hebron massacres 29 Palestinians praying in the mosque at the Tomb of the Patriarchs. Shortly thereafter the first Palestinian suicide bomber blows himself up inside Israel.

1994. The Palestinian National Authority (PNA) is established in Gaza and the West Bank. The PLO and Yassir Arafat arrive in Gaza. Jordan and Israel sign a peace treaty.

1995. Prime Minister Rabin is assassinated in Tel Aviv by an Israeli fundamentalist opposed to Oslo Accords.

1997. Israel starts building a settlement, Har Homa, on a hill overlooking East Jerusalem; widespread protests result. Israel imposes closures on Palestinian communities in the West Bank and Gaza.

2000. Israeli troops pull out of Lebanon. Israeli Prime Minister Ehud Barak, Palestinian Chairman Yassir Arafat, and US President Bill Clinton meet at Camp David in a failed attempt to negotiate a settlement on final status issues. The Al-Aqsa Intifada begins following a visit to the Temple Mount/Haram al-Sharif by Israeli opposition leader Ariel Sharon. The violence escalates rapidly and continues, involving rock-throwing, machine

gun and mortar fire, suicide bombings, and road ambushes.

2001. Negotiations at Taba, Egypt, are unsuccessful.

2002. The Arab League (22 countries) proposes peace, normal relations, and regional integration with Israel in exchange for an end to the Occupation and a "just solution" to the refugee problem. Israel rejects the offer and begins unilateral construction of the Wall. In retaliation for a series of suicide bombings, the Israeli army reoccupies areas of the West Bank. Yassir Arafat is placed under house arrest.

2002-2003. The "Quartet" (US, UN, EU, Russia) develops "Roadmap to Peace." Palestinians pledge full support; Israel agrees but with 14 "reservations" that render it ineffective.

2004. Two Hamas leaders are killed in separate Israeli air strikes. Yassir Arafat dies.

2005. Israel evacuates 8,000 settlers from Gaza and constructs housing for 13,000 more settlers in the West Bank. Israeli troops withdraw from Gaza but retain control of crossings, airspace, and coastline.

2006. Hamas wins democratic legislative elections after holding to a unilateral ceasefire for more than a year. US and EU cut off aid and declare embargo on Palestinian government. Sharon suffers massive stroke, and Olmert assumes power. Gaza militants kill two Israeli soldiers and capture one; Israel launches a five-month attack on Gaza.

2007. Hamas and Fatah militants fight each other for control of Gaza. Annapolis Peace Conference launches unsuccessful one-year effort to achieve peace before the end of the Bush Administration.

2008-2009. Israel launches 22-day assault on Gaza. The official purpose, questioned by many Israelis, is to eradicate Hamas and stop rocket attacks.

Resources for further study

Many of the resources listed below were consulted in the preparation of this book. For a complete list of sources and citations used in this document, please visit IsraelPalestineMissionNetwork.org.

Books and Reports

Amnesty International (June 2007) *Enduring Occupation, Palestinians Under Siege in the West Bank*

Ateek, Naim Stifan (2009) *A Palestinian Christian Cry for Reconciliation*

Aruri, Naseer (2003) *Dishonest Broker: The US Role in Israel and Palestine*

Baltzer, Anna (2007) *Witness in Palestine*

Bennis, Phyllis (2007) *Understanding the Palestinian-Israeli Conflict: A Primer*

Benvenisti, Meron (2002) *Sacred Landscape: The Buried History of the Holy Land since 1948*

Burg, Avraham (2008) *The Holocaust is Over; We Must Rise from Its Ashes*

Burge, Gary (2003) *Whose Land? Whose Promise?*

Carter, Jimmy (2006) *Palestine: Peace not Apartheid*

Chacour, Elias (1984) *Blood Brothers*

Chacour, Elias (1990) *We Belong to the Land*

Chapman, Colin (1983) *Whose Promised Land: Israel or Palestine?*

Chavits, Zev (2007) *A Match Made in Heaven*

Christison, Kathleen (2001) *Perceptions of Palestine: Their Influence on U.S. Middle East Policy*

Cook, Jonathan (2008) *Disappearing Palestine: Israel's Experiments in Human Despair*

Curtiss, Richard H. (1990) *Stealth PACs: Lobbying Congress for Control of U.S. Middle East Policy.* Washington, DC: The American Educational Trust

Marda Dunsky (2008) *Pens and Swords: How the American Mainstream Media Report the Israeli-Palestinian Conflict*

Ellis, Marc (1990) *Beyond Innocence and Redemption*

Findley, Paul (1993) *Deliberate Deceptions: Facing the Facts about the U.S.-Israel Relationship* Washington, DC: The American Educational Trust

Findley, Paul (1985) *They Dare To Speak Out: People and Institutions Confront Israel's Lobby*

Friedman, Thomas L. (1989) *From Beirut to Jerusalem*

Gorenberg, Gershom (2006) *The Accidental Empire: Israel and the Birth of the Settlements, 1967-1977*

Grodzinsky, Yosef (2004) *In the Shadow of the Holocaust*

Halper, Jeff (2008) *An Israeli in Palestine*

Karpf, Anne et al. (2008) *A Time to Speak Out: Independent Jewish Voices on Israel, Zionism and Jewish Identity*

Khalidi, Walid (1992) *All that Remains: The Palestinian Villages Occupied and Depopulated by Israel in 1948*

Mary Elizabeth King (2007) *A Quiet Revolution: The First Palestinian Intifada and Non-violent Resistance*

Lindsey, Hal (1970) *The Late, Great Planet Earth*

Makdisi, Saree (2008) *Palestine Inside Out*

Mearsheimer, John L. and Walt, Stephen M. (2007) *The Israel Lobby and US Foreign Policy*

Miller, Aaron David (2008) *The Much Too Promised Land: America's Elusive Search for Arab-Israeli Peace*

Morris, Benny (1987) *The Birth of the Palestinian Refugee Problem, 1947-1949*

Nathan, Susan (2005) *The Other Side of Israel: My Journey Across the Jewish/Arab Divide*

Pappe, Ilan (2006) *The Ethnic Cleansing of Palestine*

Qumsiyeh, Mazin (2004) *Sharing the Land of Canaan:*

Human rights and the Israeli-Palestinian Struggle

Said, Edward (2000) *Out of Place*

Sharp, Jeremy M. (January 2008) "US Foreign Aid to Israel." Congressional Research Service Report for Congress, Prepared for members and committees of Congress

Sizer, Stephen (2004) *Christian Zionism: Roadmap to Armageddon?*

Tolan, Sandy (2006) *The Lemon Tree: An Arab, A Jew, and the Heart of the Middle East*

Wagner, Don (2003) *Dying in the Land of Promise: Palestine and Palestinian Christianity from Pentecost–2000*

Weber, Timothy P. (2004) *On the Road to Armageddon*

Zertal, Edith and Eldar, Akiva (2007) *Lords of the Land: The War over Israel's Settlements in the Occupied Territories*

Zunes, Stephen (2002) *Tinderbox: US Middle East Policy and the Roots of Terrorism*

Films and DVDs

Cup Final (1991)

Jerusalem: The East Side Story (2008)

Occupation 101 (2007)

Paradise Now (2005)

Peace, Propaganda, and the Promised Land (2006)

Salt of this Sea (2008)

The Iron Wall (2006)

Steadfast Hope, the companion DVD

This resource includes a DVD with eight segments.

- Introduction: A Tale of Two Peoples (11 mins.)
- Chapter 1: The Big Picture (11 mins.)
- Chapter 2: Can We Call It Apartheid? (9 mins.)
- Chapter 3: Non-violent Resistance (8 mins.)
- Chapter 4: Who Profits? (11 mins.)
- Chapter 5: Telling the Story (9 mins.)
- Chapter 6: Hardships and Hope (15 mins.)
- Conclusion: Transformation (4 mins.)

The booklet and DVD can be used for individual learning and reflection, but, as with most curricula, participants will gain more if they are able to interact and share what they learn with others.

To order the booklet and the free DVD, contact the Israel/Palestine Mission Network of the Presbyterian Church (U.S.A.) at ipmnletter@yahoo.com.

A leader's guide to using this resource

Practical strategies for successful discussion leadership

Creating a space for open, safe conversation occurs as you set the tone by being a non-anxious presence and example for those present. *Remember that the tenor of the first encounter sets the stage for those that follow.*

Be clear with your participants about the amount of time you expect to be together. Your role as the presenter and leader means that you may act as a moderator if participants too quickly take sides in the conversation. You may also wish to be specific about your expectations for honorable speech with one another in claiming one's own positions and responding to the readings.

Make sure that everyone gets to share before others share for a second time. Be sure to preserve time for your group to process what they have seen and consider what it is God may be calling them to do with what they are learning.

Make sure you have a comfortable space for the presentation and conversation where all can see and hear who is speaking. If you are able, display a large post-1967 map of Israel/Palestine to help in identifying the places discussed in the materials. Finally, painful experience teaches that it is always wise to test your DVD player and screen ahead of each class.

The three-part meeting format works well in studying challenging or controversial material:

1. Begin by recognizing God's presence in your midst with a prayer. Depending on your group, it may be necessary to set the stage for a time of conversation and sharing by providing a 15- to 20-minute overview of the range of materials. This can be accomplished by a combination of the DVD visuals provided and a spoken overview of the reading that has been assigned. This practice is especially helpful for those who may have done

Alvin Huie

Keep Hope Alive is a Peacemaking program of three San Francisco Bay Area Presbyteries, in partnership with the YMCA of East Jerusalem and the YWCA of Palestine. Each year, two delegations go to the West Bank to help Palestinian families plant olive trees (February) and harvest olives (October). The presence of internationals can help Palestinians avoid confrontation with armed Israeli settlers who seek to prevent the Palestinians' planting and harvesting on their land, thereby depriving Palestinians of their primary source of income.

their reading weeks before and those catching up with the conversation.

2. Next, elicit from the participants what was new or surprising to them in the materials and presentation. This will help you locate where the participants are in their understanding of the issues. Don't underestimate the power of this step as the more introverted participants may take a while longer than the extroverted ones to feel safe sharing their voice and thoughts with the group.

3. Finally, offer some "digging deeper" questions, such as those suggested on the next page. If you feel at ease with the materials and topic, it may be tempting to begin answering the questions at this point. Instead, see if you can draw out differing responses from the members of your group. Remember, you are trying to provide a safe space for the participants to hear the resource and each other, with the hope that they will be ready to respond in the way the Holy Spirit invites. Finish

with the assignment for the next week and a closing prayer.

As with other topics of exploration, the Israeli-Palestinian conflict can bring out strong feelings and reactions. The Peacemaking Program has multiple resources that help congregations with such conversations, including "To Strengthen Christ's Body: Tools for Talking about Tough Issues" (PDS Item #2435808001).

Planning to lead a study-discussion group in your church

This book and the accompanying DVD are designed for individual use or within a one-week or multi-week church adult education curriculum:

A one-week conversation

Hand out copies of the booklet and DVD one to two weeks in advance so participants have enough time to watch the DVD as a feature film and read through the entire 48- page booklet. Because of time limitations, you will have to decide what part of the booklet to emphasize. Chapter 1 of the DVD, "The Big Picture," is recommended. You can use the three-part meeting guide described on the previous page or tailor your time together based on the level of exposure your participants have on this topic.

A four-week series

- **Week 1**
  Welcome and orientation; the Christian call to peacemaking
- **Week 2**
  Booklet: Introduction and Part One
  DVD: Introduction
- **Week 3**
  Booklet: Part Two
  DVD: Chapters 1, 2, 3, 6
- **Week 4**
  Booklet: Part Three
  DVD: Chapters 4, 5, Conclusion

A seven-week series

- **Week 1**
  Booklet: pages 1-3
  DVD: Introduction
- **Week 2**
  Booklet: pages 4-11
  DVD: Chapter 1
- **Week 3**
  Booklet: pages 12-19
  DVD: Chapter 5

- **Week 4**
  Booklet: pages 20-27
  DVD: Chapter 2
- **Week 5**
  Booklet: pages 28-33
  DVD: Chapter 3

- **Week 6**
  Booklet: pages 34-39
  DVD: Chapter 4
- **Week 7**
  Booklet: pages 40-42, 44
  DVD: Chapter 6 and Conclusion

"Digging deeper" questions to encourage productive group discussion

- What is your narrative of the Israeli-Palestinian conflict. Why?
- What does peacemaking mean to you?
- Is it easy for you to take sides in armed conflicts. Why, or why not?
- Some would say that this conflict is too complex to understand fully. In what ways is it simple to understand?
- How is the voice of the American media consistent or divergent from what has been presented in this study?
- How does the religious and ethnic diversity in Israel/Palestine hinder or aid the prospect for peace?

- What does the holy city of Jerusalem mean to you as a Christian? To Jews? To Muslims? To local Christians in Palestine/Israel?
- How does seeing the Israeli-Palestinian conflict as a recent phenomenon, rather than as an ancient religious conflict, help give you hope that peace is possible?
- What is the closest metaphor for the settlements in modern history?
- What would you do if you were cut off from a portion of your county or state and could not get to school, work, or civic events?
- What would you do if civilians in a neighboring country were being targeted by armed forces?

- What natural resources do you take for granted? What would you do if you were no longer granted access to those resources?
- For you, is physically violent resistance to injustice ever permissible?
- What will need to happen for a just peace to come about between Palestinians and Israelis?
- Do you profit through injustice in any of your investments? How do you know?
- In light of what you have learned through this study about what others are doing, what can you and your congregation do?

Sameh A. Habeeb

David Young

These boys in the Gaza Strip and young woman in the West Bank have lived their entire lives under occupation. May their steadfast hope in a better future be ours, too.